The
Scuppernong Press

Wake Forest, NC

An Ordinary Commentary by Ordinary Men:

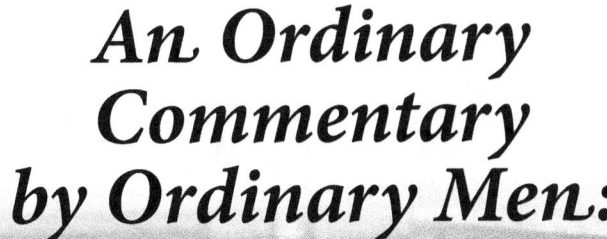

The Sermon on the Mount

Richard Lee Montgomery
M. A. (R. E.), D. R. E

Commentators:

Lyman Abbott, Joseph Addison Alexander, Albert Barnes, Dietrich Bonhoeffer, John Albert Broadus, Thomas Boston, David Brown, William Bruce, William Burkitt, James Glenworth Butler, John Calvin, Oswald Chambers, George Whitefield Clark, Adam Clarke, Howard Crosby, Philip Doddridge, Charles John Ellicott, Charles Rosenbury Erdman, Andrew Fuller, John Gill, Harvey Goodwin, John Guyse, James Hastings, Matthew Henry, Daniel Harvey Hill, Martin Luther, Thomas Manton, Alexander Mclaren, William McIntyre, George Campbell Morgan, James Morrison, William Nast, Simon Patrick, Edwin Wilbur Rice, Legh Richmond, Archibald Thomas Robertson, John Charles Ryle, Charles Frederick Schaeffer, Philip Schaff, Charles Haddon Spurgeon, John Bird Sumner, David Thomas, Henry Thornton, John Heyl Vincent

An Ordinary Commentary by Ordinary Men: The Sermon on the Mount

©2020 Richard Lee Montgomery

First Printing

The Scuppernong Press
PO Box 1724
Wake Forest, NC 27588
www.scuppernongpress.com

Cover and book design by Frank B. Powell, III

All rights reserved. Printed in the United States of America.

No part of this book may be reproduced or transmitted in any form or by any means, electronic or mechanical, including photocopying, recording, or by any information and storage and retrieval system, without written permission from the editor and/or publisher.

International Standard Book Number ISBN 978-1-942806-30-1

Library of Congress Control Number: 2020921395

Contents

Foreword i

Brief Biographies iii

Sermon Introduction 1

Chapter 5 5

The Crowds Come to Hear Jesus, 5:1-2 5
Jesus Teaching the Beatitudes, 5:3-12 9
Salt and Light, 5:13-16 19
Fulfilling the Law, 5:17-20 23
Personal Relationship — Murder, 5:21-26 27
Personal Relationship — Adultery, 5:27-30 31
Personal Relationship — Divorce, 5:31-32 33
Personal Relationship — Oaths, 5:33-37 35
Personal Relationship — Eye for an Eye, 5:38-42 37
Personal Relationship — Love Your Enemies, 5:43-48 41

Chapter 6 45

Types of Righteousness and Religion, 6:1-18 45
Righteousness and Ordinary Earthly Things, 6:19-34 55

Chapter 7 65

Christ Admonishes Thoughtless Judgment, 7:1-6 65
True Prayer and the Golden Rule, 7:7-12 69
Social Morality and the Divine View of Life, 7:13-14 71
The Elements of Moral Character and Its Fruit, 7:15-20 73
Man's Religions, and Their Testing Day, 7:21-27 77
The World's Greatest Teacher, 7:28-29 81

Commentaries 83

Foreword

The hope and desire for this commentary is that it might bring to your life, a stronger hope and direction in your relationship to Jesus Christ, as your Lord and Savior. The lifestyle motivation for all born again believers ought to commence each morning with the desire to serve Christ with one result, that God would be glorified in your life for that day. That means what you say, how you respond to others and how you view each circumstance of any day, is that Christ would be seen in your life. Romans 12:1-2 reminds us of this kind of life: *"Therefore I urge you, brethren, by the mercies of God, to present your bodies a living and holy sacrifice, acceptable to God, which is your spiritual service of worship. ²And do not be conformed to this world, but be transformed by the renewing of your mind, so that you may prove what the will of God is, that which is good and acceptable and perfect."* [1] That is the designed lifestyle for the born again believer and when that is the saints life lived out, the hope is that Christ is magnified to a lost and dying people and that they will become mortified of their spiritual state — and see their need for the Saviour — Jesus Christ.

James Hastings states that the root meaning of a Bible commentary is the exercise *"'to search out,' 'investigate,' 'explore'; as applied to Scripture..."* [2] The sole purpose for this book is to point you always back to God's Word — the Bible. Yes, these commentator's will express their comments but at the root of their comments is Scripture. As with the other Reformers, John Calvin held to the principle that scripture interprets scripture. In this little book you will read from men or simply put, ordinary men but men who strived to grown in Godliness. Men who grew in sage, meaning those saints who grew in wisdom developing sound discernment based on their spiritual growth attained from the study of the Word of God. Men who are trustees for Christ Jesus — they can be trusted with their desires to

---

[1] *The Holy Bible, Updated New American Standard Bible* (Grand Rapids: Zondervan Publishing House, 1999), 969.
[2] James Hastings, *A Dictionary of the Bible: Dealing with its Language, Literature and Content Including the Biblical Theology, Volume 1* (A-FEAST) (New York: Charles Scribner's Sons, 1898), 459.

serve Him. It does not mean they cannot make mistakes or erroneous statements, because they can. But by and large these were men seeking to glorify their Lord.

As you prepare yourself for reading this commentary, open your Bible and turn to Matthew 5:1 and begin reading a verse or passage or even the whole chapter. Then take time to ponder or meditate on what you have just read. Then evaluate your meditative thoughts to the words and comments of these ordinary men. Then turn your eyes back to the Bible, making sure it mirror's the Word of God.

May God bless you as you study and seek to grow in God's Word.

— Richard Lee Montgomery

Brief Biographies

Lyman Abbott: Born December 18, 1835, Roxbury, Boston, Massachusetts and died October 22, 1922, New York. Graduated from the New York University. Congregational.

Joseph Addison Alexander: Born April 24, 1809, Philadelphia, Pennsylvania and died, January 28, 1860 at Princeton, New Jersey. Graduated from the College of New Jersey (Princeton University). Presbyterian.

Albert Barnes: Born December 1, 1798, Rome, New York, and died December 24, 1870, Philadelphia, Pennsylvania. Graduated from Hamilton College, Clinton, New York and Princeton Theological Seminary. Presbyterian.

Dietrich Bonhoeffer: Born February 4, 1906, Breslau, Germany and executed on April 9, 1945 at the Nazi Flossenburg Concentration Camp, Bavaria. Graduated from the University of Tubingen and Berlin University. Lutheran.

John Albert Broadus: Born January 24, 1827 in Culpeper County, Virginia and died March 16, 1895, Louisville, Kentucky. Graduated from the University of Virginia. Baptist.

Thomas Boston: Born March 17, 1676, Duns, Scotland and died May 20, 1732, Ettrick. Graduating from Edinburgh University. Presbyterian

David Brown: Born August 17, 1803, Aberdeen, Scotland and died July 3, 1897, Aberdeen. Graduated from Aberdeen University. Presbyterian.

William Bruce: Born July 30, 1757, Dublin, Ireland and died February 27, 1841, Dublin. Graduated from Trinity College, Dublin. Presbyterian.

William Burkitt: Born July 25, 1650, Hitcham, Suffolk, England and died, October 24, 1703 in Essex, England. Graduated from Pembroke College, Cambridge. Anglican.

James Glenworth Butler: Born August 3, 1821, Brooklyn, New York and died, December 29, 1916, Morris County, New Jersey. from the Yale Theological Seminary. Presbyterian.

John Calvin: Born July 10, 1509, Noyon, France and died, May 27, 1564, Geneva, Switzerland. Graduated from the University of Paris. French Protestant.

Oswald Chambers: Born July 24, 1874, Aberdeen, Scotland and died November 15, 1917, Cairo, Egypt. Educated at Dunoon College near Glasgow. Baptist.

George Whitefield Clark: Born February 15, 1831, South Orange, New Jersey and died November 10, 1911, Highstown, New Jersey. Graduated from Amherst College and Rochester Theological Seminary. Baptist.

Adam Clarke: Born 1760 or 1762, Moybeg, County Londonary (Northern Ireland) and died in London on August 26, 1832. Methodist.

Howard Crosby: Born February 27, 1826, New York City and died March 29, 1891, New York City. Graduated from New York University. Presbyterian.

Philip Doddridge: Born June 26, 1702, London, England and died October 26, 1751, Lisbon, Portugal. Educated at Kindgston-upon-Thames and St. Albans. Congregational.

Charles John Ellicott: Born April 25, 1819, Whitwell, Rutland, England and died October 15, 1905, Birchington-on-Sea, Kent, England. Educated at Stamford School and St John's College, Cambridge. Anglican.

Charles Rosenbury Erdman: Born July 20, 1866, Fayetteville, New York and died 1960, Princeton, New Jersey. Graduated from the College of New Jersey (now Princeton University) and Seminary. Presbyterian.

Andrew Fuller: Born February 6, 1754, Wicken, Cambridgeshire, England and died May 7, 1815, Kettering. No formal education. Baptist.

John Gill: Born November 23, 1697, Kettering, Northamptonshire, England and died October 14, 1771, London. Graduated from Marischal College and the University at Aberdeen. Baptist.

Harvey Goodwin: Born October 9, 1818, King's Lynn, England and died November 25, 1891, Bishopthorpe. He graduated from Cambridge in 1840 (BA) and 1843 (MA). Anglican.

John Guyse: Born 1680, Hertford, England and died November 22, 1761, Hertford. Educated at the Academy of the Rev. John Payne at Saffron Walden and the University at Aberdeen. Independent.

James Hastings: Born March 26, 1852, Huntly, Aberdeenshire, Scotland and died October 15, 1922, Aberdeen, Aberdeenshire. Graduated from the University of Aberdeen. Presbyterian.

Matthew Henry: Born October 18, 1662, Flintshire, Wales and died June 22, 1714, Cheshire, England. Attended the Academy at Islington, London. Nonconformist Puritan.

Daniel Harvey Hill: Born July 12, 1821, York County, South Carolina and died, September 24, 1889, Charlotte, North Carolina. Graduated from the United States Military Academy. Presbyterian.

Martin Luther: Born November 10, 1483, Eisleben, Germany and died February 18, 1546, Eisleben, Germany. Graduated from the University of Erfurt. Worked to bring about the Reformation of the Church.

Thomas Manton: Born 1620, Laurence Lydiard, England and died 1677, London. Educated at the University of Oxford, Wadham College and Hertford College. Nonconformist Puritan.

Alexander McClaren: Born February 11, 1826, Glasgow and died May 5, 1910, Manchester, England. Graduated from Stepney College in 1842. Baptist.

William McIntyre: Born March 6, 1806, Kilmonivaig, Scotland and died July 12, 1870, Sydney, Australia. Graduated from the Education: University of Glasgow. Presbyterian.

George Campbell Morgan: Born December 9, 1863, Tetbury, England and died, May 16, 1945, London. Educated at Gratton House, Cheltenham, Gloucestershire. Congregational.

James Morrison: Born February 14, 1816, Bathgate, Linlithgowshire, Scotland and died November 13, 1898, Florentine Bank, Hillhead, Glasgow. Educated at the University of Edinburgh. Presbyterian.

William Nast: Born June 15, 1807, Stuttgart, Germany and died May 16, 1899, Cincinnati, Ohio. Graduated from the University of Tubingen, Germany. Methodist.

Simon Patrick: Born September 8, 1626, Gainsborough, Lincolnshire, United Kingdom and died May 31, 1707, Ely, United Kingdom. Educated at Queens' College, Cambridge. Anglican.

Edwin Wilbur Rice: Born July 24, 1831, Kingsborough, N. Y. and died December 3, 1929, Philadelphia. Graduated from Union College, and Union Theological Seminary, New York City from 1855-57. Congregational.

Legh Richmond: Born January 29, 1772, Liverpool, England and died May 8, 1827, Turvey, England. Educated at Trinity College, Cambridge. Anglican.

Archibald Thomas Robertson: Born November 6, 1863, Chatham, Virginia and died September 24, 1934, Louisville, Kentucky. Graduated from Wake Forest College, North Carolina and the Southern Baptist Theological. Baptist.

John Charles Ryle: Born May 10, 1816, Macclesfield, England and died June 10, 1900, Lowestoft. Graduated from Eton College and the University of Oxford. Anglican.

Charles Frederick Schaeffer: Born September 3, 1807, Germantown, Pennsylvania and died November 23, 1879, Philadelphia. Educated at the University of Pennsylvania. Lutheran.

Philip Schaff: Born January 1, 1819, Chur, Switzerland and died October 20, 1893, New York, New York. Educated at the universities of Tubingen, Halle, and Berlin. German Reformed.

Charles Haddon Spurgeon: Born June 19, 1834, Kelvedon, Essex, England and died January 31, 1892, Menton, Alpes-Maritimes, France. No formal education beyond Newmarket Academy. Baptist.

John Bird Sumner: Born February 25, 1780, Kenilworth, Warwickshire, Great Britain and died September 6, 1862,
Addington, Surrey, United Kingdom. Graduated from Eton College and King's College. Anglican.

David Thomas: Born 1813, Pembrokeshire, England and died December 30, 1894, Ramsgate. Educated at Newport-Pagnell. Congregational.

Henry Thornton: Born March 10, 1760, London, England and died January 16, 1815, London. Attended the school at Wandsworth Common, and later at Point Pleasant, Wandsworth. Anglican.

John Heyl Vincent: Born February 23, 1832, Tuscaloosa, Alabama and died May 9, 1920, Portville, New York. Graduated from Wesleyan Institute, Newark, New Jersey. Methodist.

An Ordinary Commentary by Ordinary Men: The Sermon on the Mount

Sermon Introduction

As an introduction to the Sermon on the Mount taught by the Master Teacher, I take you to **Martin Luther's** comments: *"I AM truly glad that my exposition of the three chapters of St. Matthew, which St. Augustine calls the Lord's Sermon on the Mount, are about to be published, hoping that by the grace of God it may help to preserve and maintain the true, sure and Christian understanding of this teaching of Christ, because these sayings and texts are so very common and so often used throughout all Christendom. For I do not doubt that I have herein presented to my friends, and all others who care for these things, the true, pure Christian meaning of the same."* [3]

Oswald Chambers reminds us of a most important element in the sermon: *"In order to understand the Sermon on the Mount, it is necessary to have the mind of the Preacher, and this knowledge can be gained by anyone who will receive the Holy Spirit. (see Luke 40:13, John 20:22, Acts 19:2). The Holy Ghost is the only expounder of the teachings of Jesus. The one abiding method of interpretation of the teachings of Jesus is the Spirit of Jesus in the heart of a believer applying His principles to the particular circumstances in which he is placed. Be renewed in the spirit of your mind, says Paul, that you may make out what is that good and acceptable and perfect will of God.*

Beware of placing Our Lord as Teacher first instead of as Saviour. That tendency is prevalent to-day, and it is a dangerous tendency. We must know Him first as Saviour before His teaching has any meaning for us, or before it has any meaning other than that of an ideal which leads to despair. Fancy coming to men and women with defective lives and

---

[3] Martin Luther, *Commentary on the Sermon on the Mount* (Philadelphia: Lutheran Publication Society, 1892), v-vi.

defiled hearts and wrong main springs and telling them to be pure in heart! What is the use of giving us an ideal we cannot possibly attain? We are happier without knowing it. If Jesus is only a Teacher, then all He can do is to tantalize us by erecting a standard we cannot come anywhere near. But if we know Him first as Saviour, by being born again from above, we know that He did not come to teach us only: He came to make us what He teaches we should be. The Sermon on the Mount is a statement of the life we will live when the Holy Spirit is having His way with us.

The Sermon on the Mount must produce despair in the natural man; and that is the very thing Jesus means it to do, because immediately we get to despair we are willing to come to Jesus as paupers and to receive from Him. 'Blessed are the poor in spirit' — that is the first principle of the Kingdom. So long as we have a conceited, self-righteous notion that we can do the thing if God will help us, God has to allow us to go on until we break the neck of our ignorance over some obstacle, then we are willing to come and receive from Him. The bedrock in Jesus Christ's Kingdom is poverty, not possession; not decisions for Jesus Christ, but a sense of absolute futility 'I cannot begin to do it.' Then, says Jesus, 'Blessed are you.' That is the entrance, and it does take us a long while to believe we are poor. The knowledge of our own poverty brings us to the moral frontier where Jesus Christ works" [4]

This teaching of Jesus known as the Sermon on the Mount is recorded in the Gospel of Matthew 5-7 and similar teaching can also be found in Luke 6:17–49. In both gospel accounts we learn that this teaching is taking place early in Jesus' public ministry. It contains some of his best-known teaching and instruction for all of life. At the start of the sermon, there are fixed lessons to be drawn from in the first twelve verses known as the "Beatitudes," with the explanation of the persevering lifestyle of a Christians. The first lesson in these twelve verses is that the Christian is to live out these listed characteristics with a driving affection for God Jehovah, through Jesus Christ that He might be glorified. Another very important foundational lesson is to understand is that these descriptions are not natural tendencies.

---

[4] Oswald Chambers, *Studies in the Sermon on the Mount* (London: Simpkin Marshall, LTD, 1900), i-ii.

And finally, these fixed verses give clarity to the born-again believer to understand the complete difference between the Christian and the non-Christian.

The Sermon on the Mount is very clear with authority in these teachings of Christ about life in the Kingdom of God. The theme identified in this sermon is righteousness — not just any righteousness but the righteousness Jesus Christ. Also, very important is that when Jesus the Christ (the Anointed One) is speaking to His disciples, He is also speaking to a much larger gathering of people, with great purpose and intention. Yes, the message is to the disciples, but Jesus also desires for the message to be heard and understood by all.

An Ordinary Commentary by Ordinary Men: The Sermon on the Mount

Chapter 5

The Crowds Come to Hear Jesus
Jesus Sets the Stage for What was About to Happen.
Matthew 5:1-2

Alexander Maclaren—Verse 1a: "The unnamed mountain somewhere on the sea of Galilee is the Sinai of the new covenant. The contrast between the savage desolation of the wilderness and the smiling beauty of the sunny slope near the haunts of men symbolizes the contrast in the genius of the two codes, given from each. There God came down in majesty, and the cloud hid Him from the people's gaze; here Jesus sits amidst His followers, God with us.  The King proclaims the fundamental laws of His kingdom and reveals much of its nature by the fact that He begins by describing the characteristics of its subjects, as well as by the fact that the description is cast in the form of beatitudes.

We must leave unsettled the question as to the relation between the Sermon on the Mount and the shorter edition of part of it given by Luke, only pointing out that in this first part of Matthew's Gospel we are evidently presented with general summaries; as, for example, the summary of the Galilean ministry in the previous verses, and the grand procession of miracles, which follows in chapters eight and nine. It is therefore no violent supposition that here too the evangelist has brought together, as specimens of our Lord's teaching, words which were not all spoken at the same time. His description of the Galilean ministry in Matthew 4:23, as 'teaching' and 'healing,' governs the arrangement of His materials from chapter five to the end of chapter nine. First comes the sermon, then the miracles follow." [5]

---

[5] Alexander Maclaren, *The Gospel of St. Matthew, Volume 1* (London: Hodder & Stoughton, 1892), 63-64.

Archibald Thomas Robertson—Verse 1b: "Seeing the crowds, Jesus went up a little higher on the mountain side above the level place where he had been healing the sick and 'sat down' as was the custom for Jewish teachers. Sat down. This was the signal that he was about to address the crowd. Cf. Lk. 4:20. Disciples came unto him. The twelve just chosen drew nearer to hear him. They felt a new sense of responsibility and privilege. Jesus had appointed them to be with him, to preach, and to have authority to cast out demons (Mk. 3:14 f.). Already they knew that they must themselves someday be preachers. Mark (3:13) comments on the fact that Jesus called whom he himself would and Luke (6:12) remarks that it was done after a night of prayer. There were other disciples present, 'a great multitude of his disciples' (Lk. 6:17), besides these twelve. There was also present a vast crowd of people from many regions all the way from Jerusalem to Tyre and Sidon (Lk. 6:17; Matt. 5:1; 7:28; 8:1). Both Matthew and Luke describe the audience as composed of both believers in Jesus and a great multitude besides." [6]

George Campbell Morgan — Verse 1c: "As he began there was a strange and wonderful attractiveness to Him, and the multitudes gathered round Him. The unfit people of all the countryside were attracted to Him. Probable the people in that district had no idea how many unfit and incompetent people there were in their midst until Jesus, moving through the towns and villages, drew them round Himself. We cannot too often read these or to solemnly consider them and catch there meaning — They brought unto Him all that were sick, holden with divers diseases and torments, possessed with devils, and epileptic and palsied, and He headed them.' But nor merely such. They crowed after Him, from Decapolis, from Galilee, from Jerusalem, from Judea and beyond Jordan." [7]

---

[6] A. T. Robertson, *Commentary on the Gospel According to Matthew* (New York: The MacMillan Company, 1911), 91.

[7] G. Campbell Morgan, *The Gospel According to Matthew* (New York: Fleming H. Revel, 1939), 37.

John Gill — **Verse 2:** *And he opened his mouth.* "He spoke with a clear and strong voice, that all the people might hear him; and with great freedom, utterance, and cheerfulness, and things of the greatest moment and importance; and taught them; not his disciples only, but the whole multitude, who heard him with astonishment. Some things in the following discourse are directed to the disciples in particular, and others regard the multitude in general." [8]

---

[8] John Gill, *An Exposition of the New Testament in Which the Sense of the Sacred Text is Given, Volume 1* (London: Mathews & Leigh, 1809), 36.

An Ordinary Commentary by Ordinary Men: The Sermon on the Mount

Jesus Teaching the Beatitudes
Component in This Lesson on the Beatitudes From Christ.
Matthew 5:3-12

Matthew Henry—Verse 3: *"Do we ask then who are happy? It is answered, 1. The poor in spirit are happy. There is a poor spiritedness that is so far from making men blessed, that it is a sin and a snare—cowardice and base fear, and a willing subjection to the lusts of men. But this poverty of spirit is a gracious disposition of soul, by which we are emptied of self, in order to our being filled with Jesus Christ. To be poor in spirit, is, 1. To be contentedly poor, willing to be empty of worldly wealth, if God orders that to be our lot; to bring our mind to our condition, when it is a low condition. Many are poor in the world, but high in spirit, poor and proud, murmuring and complaining, and blaming their lot, but we must accommodate ourselves to our poverty, must know how to be abased, Phil. 4.12. Acknowledging the wisdom of God in appointing us to poverty, we must be easy in it, patiently bear the inconveniences of it, be thankful for what we have, and make the best of that which is. It is to sit loose to all worldly wealth, and not set our hearts upon it, but cheerfully to bear losses and disappointments, which may befall us in the most prosperous state. It is not, in pride or pretense, to make ourselves poor, by throwing away what God has given us, especially as those in the church of Rome, who vow poverty, and yet engross the wealth of nations; but, if we be rich in the world, we must be poor in spirit, that is, we must condescend to the poor, and sympathize with them, as being touched with the feeling of their infirmities; we must expect and prepare for poverty; must not inordinately fear or shun it, but must bid it welcome, especially when it comes upon us for keeping a good conscience, Heb. 10.34. Job was poor in spirit, when he blessed God in taking away, as well as giving. 2. It is to be humble and lowly in our own eyes. To be poor in spirit, is to think meanly of ourselves, of what we are, and have, and do; the poor are often taken in the Old Testament for the humble*

and self-denying, as opposed to those that are at ease, and the proud; it is to be as little children in our opinion of ourselves, weak, foolish, and insignificant, ch. 18.4.—19.14. Laodicea was poor in spirituals, wretchedly and miserably poor, and yet rich in spirit, so well increased with goods, as to have need of nothing, Rev. 3.1. On the other hand, Paul was rich in spirituals, excelling most in gifts and graces, and yet poor in spirit, the least of the apostles, less than the least of all saints, and nothing in his own account. It is to look with a holy contempt upon ourselves, to value others, and undervalue ourselves in comparison of them. It is to be willing to make ourselves cheap, and mean, and little, to do good; to become all things to all men. It is to acknowledge that God is great, and we are mean; that he is holy, and we are sinful; that he is all, and we are nothing, less than nothing, worse than nothing; and to humble ourselves before him, and under his mighty hand. 3. It is to come off from all confidence in our own righteousness and strength, that we may depend only upon the merit of Christ for our justification, and the Spirit and grace of Christ for our sanctification. That broken and contrite spirit with which the publican cried for mercy to a poor sinner, is this poverty of spirit. We must call ourselves poor, because always in want of God's grace, always begging at God's door, always hanging on in his house.

Now, (1.) This poverty in spirit is put first among the Christian graces. The philosophers did not reckon humility among their moral virtues, but Christ puts it first. Self-denial is the first lesson to be learned in his school, and poverty of spirit entitled to the first beatitude. The foundation of all other graces is laid in humility. Those who would build high, must begin low; and it is an excellent preparative for the entrance of gospel-grace into the soul; it fits the soil to receive the seed. Those who are weary and heavy laden, are the poor in spirit, and they shall find rest with Christ.

(2.) They are blessed. Now they are so, in this world. God looks graciously upon them. They are his little ones and have their angels. To them he gives more grace; they live the most comfortable lives, and are easy to themselves and all about them, and nothing comes amiss to them; while high spirits are always uneasy.

(3.) Theirs is the kingdom of heaven. The kingdom of grace is composed of such; they only are fit to be members of Christ's church, which is called the congregation of the poor; (Ps. 74.19.) the kingdom of glory is prepared for them. Those who thus humble themselves, and comply with God when he humbles them, shall be thus exalted. The great, high spirits go away with the glory of the kingdoms of the earth; but the humble, mild, and yielding souls obtain the glory of the kingdom of heaven. We are ready to think concerning those who are rich, and do good with their riches, that, no doubt, theirs is the kingdom of heaven; for they can thus lay up in store a good security for the time to come: but what shall the poor do, who have not wherewithal to do good? Why, the same happiness is promised to those who are contentedly poor, as to those who are usefully rich. If I am not able to spend cheerfully for his sake, if I can but want cheerfully for his sake, even that shall be recompensed. And do not we serve a good Master then?" [9]

Legh Richmond —Verse 4: *"In this that he saith, 'Blessed be they that weep,' he noteth such as do know and feel with sorrow and heaviness of conscience that they be sinners, and the filthiness of their sins maketh them sorrowful and heavy-hearted; yet shall they in Christ be comforted."* [10]

Charles Frederick Schaeffer —Verse 5: *"Blessed are the meek; for they shall inherit the earth.*

A. The meek; the Lord refers to the words in Ps. 37:11. In that psalm the godly and the wicked are contrasted. One feature of the character of the former is meekness, by which term (see 21:5) a lowly or humble mind is indicated, as in Matt. 11:29; Eph. 4:2, the opposite of a spirit of envy and strife, James 3:13, 14; Rom. 12:19. This devout frame of mind is produced in the penitent and believing sinner by a deep sense

---

[9] Matthew Henry, *An Exposition of the Old and New Testament*, Volume 5 (Philadelphia: Edward Barrington & George D. Haswell, 1825), 47-48.
[10] Legh Richmond, *A Selection from the Writings of the Reformers and Early Protestant Divines of the Church of England*, Volume 5 (London: John Hatchard, Bookseller to Her Majesty, 1810), 637.

of his unworthiness before God, and of his many sins which caused Him to mourn. It is exemplified in the Prodigal Son, Luke 15:21. —B. They shall inherit the earth — they shall not lose, but gain. The 'first commandment with promise' (Eph. 6:2) secures to children who honor their parents a long life 'upon the land, etc.,' Exod. 20:12. In this happy land the Israelites found liberty and every other temporal blessing. Hence it served as an image of all the blessings, whether temporal or spiritual, which God bestows (see Ps. 37:3, 9, 11, 22, 29; Isai. 60:21). In accordance with this view, the 'rest' which the Israelites found in the land of Canaan, is represented in Hebr. 4:1-9, as an image of the rest which awaits believers in heaven. 'To inherit the earth' (Ps. 25:13), or, strictly speaking, the land of promise (Hebr. 11:9), is therefore equivalent to the phrase, to receive fulness of joy and peace from God (see 1 Tim. 4:8, and comp. 25:34). To the meek the Lord elsewhere (11:29) promises rest for their souls. The sense is: The true disciples receive the kingdom (Luke 12: 32); they are sanctified by the Holy Spirit and made 'kings and priests unto God' (Rev. 1:6) or invested with a holy and royal (kingly) priesthood in this life already (1 Pet. 2:5, 9). When they shall be glorified in heaven (Phil. 3:21; Rom. 8:30) and behold the Saviors' glory (John 17:24), they shall be 'glad with exceeding joy' (1 Pet. 4:13), and live and reign with Christ forever, enjoying all the happiness and glory of heaven, 2 Tim. 2:12; Rom. 5:17; 8:17. Thus they inherit the heavenly land, the 'land of pure delight where saints immortal reign.'

Verse 6: *Blessed are they that hunger and thirst after righteousness: for they shall be filled.*

A. Hunger and thirst after. The bodily sensations of hunger and thirst, as images of strong desires of the soul, frequently occur in the Scriptures; Ps. 42:2; Isai. 41:17; 49:10; 55:1; 65:13; Amos 8:11; John 6:35. The Saviour satisfies the soul with the bread and water of life (John 4:10, 14;6:35). — B. Righteousness. Paul distinguishes in Phil. 3:9 two kinds of righteousness: first, human righteousness, or that external rectitude which the Jews sought after by the strict observance of the laws of Moses — the righteousness of the scribes and Pharisees, mentioned below, ver. 20, and 23:23-28; Luke 18:9; secondly, that 'righteousness which is of God by faith,' and which, in Rom. 1:17; 3:21, 22, is called the 'righteousness of God' — that which alone avails before Him, and

An Ordinary Commentary by Ordinary Men: The Sermon on the Mount

He alone bestows. It is that state of the believer to which he attains through the imputation of the merits of Christ (Rom. 4:5-8; 8:1-4; 1 John 2:2; Gal. 4:4, 5; Hebr. 10:4-14; Isai., Ch. 53). For an illustration, see Phil. 3:8-14. The believer will be 'delivered from the body of this death' (Rom. 7:24) in a future state and be clothed with perfect righteousness (2 Pet. 3:13. See above 1:19, B.; 3:15, B.). — C, They .... filled — the wants or desires of their hearts shall be fully satisfied by Him whose Spirit produced such hunger and thirst. The believer is justified and delivered from guilt and punishment by his Saviour (Rom. 3:24; 5:9); his conscience finds peace through the atonement of Christ (Rom. 5:1); his painful sense of guilt (his hunger and thirst) is relieved (Col. 1:19-22), and he gives a reason of the hope that is in him (1 Pet. 3:15) by gratefully repeating the words of Paul: 'There is therefore now no condemnation, etc.' (Rom. 8:1)." [11]

John Albert Broadus — Verse 7: *"Merciful. The original word includes also the idea of compassion, as in Heb. 2:17; Prov. 14:21, and implies a desire to remove the evils which excite compassion. It thus denotes not only mercy to the guilty, but pity for the suffering, and help to the needy. See Luke 3:11; Matt. 25:3740; James 2:13. To be merciful is not the ground of receiving mercy from God, but an occasion and condition thereof. (18:33f.) Comp. the relation between forgiving and being forgiven, as explained on 6:12. The Jerusalem Talmud gives as a saying of Gamaliel, 'Whensoever thou hast mercy, God will have mercy upon thee; if thou hast not mercy, neither will God have mercy upon thee."* [12]

Edwin Wilbur Rice — Verse 8: *"Blessed ... the pure in heart. Closely like this is Ps. 51:10. The leaders in Jewish religion laid great stress on outward cleanness and purification; Jesus puts the great emphasis on inward purity. This does not refer chief-*

---

[11] Charles F. Schaeffer, *Annotations on the Gospel According to St. Matthew, Part 1, Matthew 1-15* (New York: Charles Scribners Sons, 1896), 93-95.

[12] John A. Broadus, *An American Commentary On the New Testament. Commentary on the Gospel of Matthew* (Philadelphia: American Baptist Publication Society, 1886), 91.

ly to chastity as Romish interpreters imply. It calls for purity from all forms of sin in the thought. It requires sincerity, truthfulness, chastity, love of God; in fact all that included in a 'new heart.' The pure possess the spiritual eye that will see God." [13]

Harvey Goodwin — Verse 9: *"Blessed are the peacemakers — that is, not merely, blessed are they who are of a humble quiet peaceable disposition, though no doubt such persons are in a very high degree blessed, but blessed are they who cause peace and goodwill to prevail amongst men, who are able and who strive by their example, or their kind efforts, or (if it fall within the sphere of their duty) by their exhortations, to forward that kingdom which is emphatically a kingdom of peace. There are few blessings which our Lord could have pronounced, more suitable to the condition of His first disciples than this; it is suitable no doubt at all times, and declares in a wonderful manner, and in very few words, what ought to be the principle and character of the lives of all, who wish to follow Him in spirit and in truth; but to the first disciples there would seem to be a still more striking fitness, because the virtue upon which the Lord pronounced His blessing was then so new in the world, and yet it was the very virtue by which the world was to be subdued and His kingdom established. If My kingdom were of this world, said our Saviour before Pontius Pilate, then would My servants fight, and S. Peter, when he saw his Master about to be taken prisoner, bethought himself at once of his sword, and Christ took the occasion even then of giving a lesson concerning the principles of His kingdom, by commanding the sword to be put in the sheath, and healing the wound which S. Peter had made. Nor is the peculiar blessing allotted to the peace makers to be omitted from our notice. They shall be called the children of God; they are most worthy of the name of children of God, who practise in their own spheres, and according to their means and ability, that conduct, which may find its example in Him, who maketh men to be of one mind in an house, who maketh wars to cease in all the world, who loves unity and looks with pleasure upon those who live in peace and godly love.*

---

[13] Edwin W. Rice, *Commentary on the Gospel According to Matthew* (Philadelphia: The American Sunday-School Union, 1897), 65.

In heathen times men had a different estimate of things: the men most like gods in their eyes were they who were the bravest in war; valour with them was virtue; the most proud and cruel and overbearing were the most heroic. Christ set us a new pattern, and taught us by His own most precious example, that he was the bravest who could forgive injuries, he most worthy of being exalted who could most completely humble himself." [14]

Daniel Harvey Hill —Verses 10-11: *"'Blessed are they which are persecuted for righteousness' sake: for theirs is the kingdom of heaven. Blessed are ye when men shall revile you, and persecute you, and say all manner of evil against you, falsely, for my sake. Rejoice and be exceeding glad; for great is your reward in heaven: for so persecuted they the prophets which were before you." 'They are to expect persecution, reviling, all manner of evil speaking. Under all these trials, they are to be concerned about two things only. First: That their lives should be so blameless as to render the accusations of their enemies groundless and false. Second: That a higher spirit than that of mere submission is to be cultivated — 'Rejoice and be exceeding glad.'*

Acquiescence in the will of God is a high attainment; but rejoicing, under the afflictive dispensations of his hand, is a grace. Philosophy has reached to the one, the other is the work of the Spirit. The gospel demands more than cold stoicism. None can mistake its teachings. 'Giving thanks always, for all things, unto God and the Father, in the name of our Lord Jesus Christ.' 'In everything give thanks: for this is the will of God in Christ Jesus concerning you.'

Persecuted, afflicted, and cast down child of God! talk not of submission. Uncomplaining Job did not dishonour his Maker, and 'charge God foolishly.' But the Lord utters his voice from amidst the thick darkness which envelopes his throne, 'Whoso offereth praise glorifieth me.' Suffering parent! hanging over the couch of a dying child, watching the colour fade from his cheek, the light grow dim in his eye; feeling the

---

[14] Harvey Goodwin, *A Commentary on the Gospel of S. Matthew* (Cambridge: Deighton, Bell & Company, 1857), 66-67.

pulse grow more and more thread-like, until your tremulous finger can no longer distinguish it. Sufferer! do you then pray to be able to say, 'The Lord gave, and the Lord hath taken away, blessed be the name of the Lord'? Rather pour out your heart in thankfulness to God that Jesus has conquered death, hell, and the grave. Rather praise him that your child has been taken from the evil to come. Duty would have awaited him here; praise will be his occupation there. The child has been called to the higher employment. Thank God for it. Two things deserve our special attention in the three verses, beginning with the 10th and ending with the 12th. First: The disciples of Christ are to expect persecution under false charges and accusations. The devil and his followers have never yet had the audacity and impudence to persecute virtue as such. They first blacken the character of the victim, and then harass, annoy, and persecute him to death. Jesus was crucified under the charge of blasphemy. Stephen was stoned to death under the same accusation. Paul and Silas were scourged and cast into prison at Philippi, for troubling the city and teaching strange customs. Socrates, the wisest and purest of the philosophers of antiquity, was poisoned for introducing new gods, and corrupting the youth. Daniel was cast into the den of lions, not for worshiping the true God, but for disobeying the king's decree. The Hebrew youth were thrown into the fiery furnace for the same reason. God has stamped so much of his own image upon our fallen race, that history records no instance of men being so depraved, as to persecute the righteous for their virtues, but always for alleged vices. The apostle truly declared, that 'all who live godly in Christ Jesus shall suffer persecution.' But the godly have always been persecuted as cheats, impostors, and hypocrites.

Second: We notice that Jesus did not deceive his disciples. He did not disguise from them that they were to expect stripes, imprisonment, cruel mockings, reviling, and death. The strongest possible argument can be drawn from this candour of the Son of God, as to the divine character of his mission. When men wish to allure others into an enterprise, they do not speak of its difficulties, dangers, hardships, and trials. Recruiting sergeants, with their drums and fifes, try to allure by 'the pride, pomp, and circumstance of war;' they never allude to the hot, weary marches, the dreary night-watches, the mangled limbs, and crushed carcasses of the battle-field. False religions have been ever *profuse in promises of temporal well-being and eternal glory, won without holiness of heart and life. Mahomet promised riches, honours, sensual indulgences and a passport to heaven, to all who followed the crescent, irrespective of their sins and pollutions. The Mormon Prophet promised wealth, ease, luxury, and licentious indulgence, to all who would acknowledge him as their spiritual guide and temporal leader. Jesus Christ promised nothing to his disciples but trials and afflictions. Poverty, contempt, a life of shame, and a death of ignominy, were to be their lot and portion. How then are we to account for the amazing success of his mission? Upon what principle can we explain the rapid spread of the gospel? In thirty years after the death of Christ, the persecution began under Nero. The historian Tacitus speaks of 'the great multitude' of Christians then at Rome. In forty years more, Pliny, the Roman governor of Pontus and Bithynia, wrote his celebrated letter to Trajan, the emperor. In it he complains that 'the contagion of this superstition had seized not only the cities, but the less towns also, and the open country, so that the temples were almost forsaken, and a long intermission of the sacred solemnities had taken place.' About one hundred years after the death of our Lord, Clemens Alexandrinus wrote that 'Christianity is spread throughout the world, in every nation, and village, and city.' What reason can we give for the wonderful triumph of the gospel in so short a time? It is no sufficient explanation to say that men will submit to any bodily torture and mental anguish to save the soul. True, the Hindoo will pierce his skin with hooks, and tear his flesh with pincers, yea, he will even allow his body to be crushed and mangled beneath the bloody wheels of the car of his idol. True, the loving mother has often given 'the fruit of her body for the sin of her soul.' The seven times heated image of Moloch has consumed ten thousands of tender babes. The turbid Ganges has often been choked with the voluntary offerings of pagan mothers. But there has always been some notoriety, some eclat, some gratification of vanity, attending the sacrifice. The disciples of Jesus were, taught, on the contrary, to expect slander instead of applause, contempt instead of glory. Again, the heathen, who immolates himself or his offspring, not only gains thereby the admiration of his countrymen, but expects to win heaven without holiness of heart. Men will endure torture, ignominy, and death, to propitiate offended Deity; they will do anything, suffer anything, to gain eternal life, except love God and keep his commandments. But*

Jesus requires his disciples not only to die for the truth, but also to live for the truth. Every child of God must not only hold himself ready to wear, if necessary, the martyr's crown, but he must also lead a consistent, holy, and useful life." [15]

Adam Clarke—Verse 12: *"Rejoice. In the testimony of a good conscience; for, without this, suffering has nothing but misery in it.*

Be exceeding glad. Leap for joy. There are several cases on record, where this was literally done by the martyrs, in Queen Mary's days. Great is your reward in heaven. In the Talmudical tract Pirkey Aboth, are these words: 'Rabbi Tarpon said, the day is short: the work is great: the labourers are slow: the reward is great: and the father of the family is urgent.'

The followers of Christ are encouraged to suffer joyfully on two considerations. 1. They are thereby conformed to the prophets who went before. 2. Their reward in heaven is a great one. God gives the grace to suffer, and then crowns that grace with glory; hence it is plain, the reward is not of debt, but of grace: Rom. 6:23." [16]

---

[15] D. H. Hill, *A Consideration of the Sermon on the Mount* (Philadelphia: William S. & Alfred Martein, 1858), 17-22.

[16] Adam Clarke, *The New Testament of Our Lord Jesus Christ, Volume 1, Matthew to the Acts* (New York: Lane & Scott, 1850), 68.

Salt and Light
Here Jesus Uses the Matter of Salt and Light to Refer to the Role of His Followers in This Fallen World.
Matthew 5:13-16

James Hastings—Verse 13: *"Ye are the salt of the earth: but if the salt have lost its savour, where with shall it be salted? it is thenceforth good for nothing, but to be cast out and trodden under foot of men.*

The exact position of these words in the Sermon on the Mount must be carefully remembered. They follow immediately after the Beatitudes those sayings in which Christ had described the various qualities of character essential to the citizen of the Kingdom of Heaven, that is, for one who would obey the rule which He had come on earth to establish and extend. A citizen of that Kingdom, Christ had just taught His hearers, must be humble-minded: he must grieve over the sin and the various evils which exist in the world; he must be gentle; he must desire righteousness above all things; he must be merciful; he must be pure-minded in the fullest sense of the words; he must do all in his power to promote peace; and he must be prepared to suffer in order that righteousness may be promoted and extended. A character which fulfils these conditions, that is, a character of which these virtues are the factors, is the character desired by Christ, and such a character is His own.

Immediately after this description has been given, as soon as ever this ideal has been set us as the standard, Christ addresses the words of the text to those who were following Him and learning from Him. To them He looked to cultivate this character. And for a moment He thinks of them, not as they actually were, but as He would have them be. For a moment He treats them as if His ideal for them were already realized in them; He does not say ye shall be, but ye are the salt of the earth. The spirit of all the united qualities commended in the Beatitudes is the salt of the life of the world. All of them meekness and humility and purity and the rest run up into two: the spirit of love and the spirit of righteousness. These, then, embodied in human life, are the salt of the earth, the salt of Churches and nations, of all forms of human activity, of thought, of imagination, of business, of the daily life of men. These keep humanity fresh and living, preserve it from corruption, and add to it the savour which secures to men their true and enduring enjoyment of life. But chiefly, in Christ's present idea, they were the freshening, purifying, preserving element in His Kingdom. [17]

Andrew Fuller —Verses 14-16: "'Ye are the light of the world.' 'This character implies that the world, notwithstanding its attainments in science, is in a state of darkness; and that the only true light that is to be found in it is that which proceedeth from Christ. It may seem too much for our Saviour to give that character to his disciples which he elsewhere claims as his own. The truth is, He, as the sun, shines with supreme lustre, and they, as the moon, derive their light from Him, and reflect it on the world. As ministers, it is for them to show unto men the way of salvation; and, as Christians, to set the example of walking in it. On this account they require to be conspicuous. There is indeed a modesty in true religion, which, so far as respects ourselves, would induce us to steal through the world, if possible, unnoticed; but this cannot be; Christians being diverse from all people in their principles and pursuits, all eyes will be upon them. They are as 'a city set upon a hill, which cannot be hid.' Their faults, as well as their excellences, will be marked both by friends and enemies. Nor is it desirable it should be otherwise. Light is not intended to be hid but exposed for the good of those about it. On this account we must even be concerned to let our light shine before men; not by any ostentatious display of ourselves, but by a practical and faithful exhibition of the nature and effects of the gospel, by which our heavenly Father is glorified. It is not merely by words, but works, that gospel light is conveyed to the consciences and hearts of men.

---

[17] James Hastings, *The Great Texts of the Bible, Volume 8 (Matthew)* (Edinburgh: T. & T. Clark, 1910), 101-102.

There is another saying of our Lord in another place, nearly a kin to this, though under a different image: 'Herein is my Father glorified, that ye bring forth much fruit: so shall ye be my disciples.' The glory of a husbandman does not arise from his fields or vines bearing fruit, but much fruit. A few ears of corn in the one, nearly choked with weeds, or here and there a branch, or a berry, on the other, while the greater part is covered with leaves only, would rather dishonour than honour them. And thus, it is in spiritual fruitfulness. A little religion often dishonours God more than none. An undecisive spirit, halting between God and the world, walking upon the confines of good and evil, now seeming to be on the side of God, and now on that of his adversaries, causes his name to be evil spoken of much more than the excesses of the irreligious. Hence, we may see the force of the rebuke to Laodicea; 'I know thy works, that thou art neither cold nor hot. So then because thou art lukewarm, and neither cold nor hot, I will spue thee out of my mouth.' It is also intimated that without bearing much fruit we are unworthy to be considered as Christ's disciples. He was indeed a fruitful bough. His life was filled with the fruits of love to God and man. It behoves us either to imitate his example or forego the profession of his name.

The glory of God being manifested by the good works of his children implies that they are all to be ascribed to him as their proper cause. Though we act, he actuates. A mind set on things too high for it may deny the consistency of this with the free agency and accountableness of creatures; but the humble Christian will turn it to a better use. 'Thou wilt ordain peace for us, for thou hast wrought all our work in us.'" [18]

---

[18] Joseph Belcher, *The Complete Works of Rev. Andrew Fuller: With A Memoir of His Life, Volume 1* (Philadelphia: American Baptist Publication Society, 1845), 566-567.

An Ordinary Commentary by Ordinary Men: The Sermon on the Mount

Fulfilling the Law
Through Jesus' Perfection, We Can Be Worthy in God's Sight.
Matthew 5:17-20

James Morison —Verse 17: *"A fresh line of thought begins here and extends to the conclusion of the chapter. It constitutes a considerable portion of the body of the Sermon on the Mount. Its purport is to tighten the bands of morality upon the consciences of our Saviour's followers. The line of thought is, as we have said, fresh, and yet it has obvious filaments of connection with the introductory matter that goes before. It presents different phases of the ethi-*  *cal characteristics that are held forth to view in the beatitudes. And it shows in what spirit the children of the kingdom of heaven are to realize for themselves the glory of being the salt of the earth and the light of the world. Think not — suppose not, imagine not — that I am come, — or more literally, that I came, namely, into the world, — to destroy the law or the prophets: Think not that I came to relax and set aside those injunctions which are the spirit and essence of the law or the prophets. By the law He meant the original and fundamental part of the Old Testament Scriptures, the Pentateuch, or Five Books of Moses. By the prophet He meant the superadded portions of the Old Testament Scriptures, which were all written by prophets, or holy men of old who spake in the name and under the influence of God. The sum total of the whole Old Testament Scripture is a many-sided unity, and may thus be considered, according to circumstances, under a variety of aspects. Here it is viewed as inculcating a lofty style of personal goodness, righteousness, or morality. And it is indisputable that the grand aim of the whole Bible, both the Old Testament and the New, is to make men good (see Matt. 7:12, 12:40; Rom. 13:8-10; Gal. 5:14). The Saviour says, 'the law or the prophets.' It was at His option either to use this disjunctive expression, or to employ the conjunctive phrase 'the law and the prophets.' If He had employed the latter He would have brought into view the oneness of the Scriptures. By using the former He brings into view* *the plurality and diversity of the classified writings which constitute the volume of the book. He had no intention of setting aside any of the principles of righteousness or true morality, whether inculcated in the law on the one hand, or exhibited and enforced in the prophets on the other. When it is said, Imagine not that I came to destroy the law or the prophets, it is assumed that there either were, or might be, afloat in the minds of many who were longing for the coming of the Messiah, notions that were quite antagonistic to the real aim of the Messiah. It is likely that not a few expected greater liberty in things moral, less restraint. They would especially desire a very large licence when engaged in fighting the Messiah's battles and overthrowing the kingdoms of the Gentiles. The word rendered to destroy means to loosen down, to dissolve, to abrogate or set oxide; to undo, as Wycliffe gives it. The same translation is given, as an alter-native version, in the Lindisfarne Gospels, to undoenne. 'Think not that I will' dispense with any of the rules of morality, prescribed by Moses, and explained 'by the prophets' (Blair). I came not to destroy, but to fulfil (both the law and the prophets): To fulfil, that is, to render full obedience to those great commandments (see ver. 19) which it is the pre-eminent aim of the Scriptures to inculcate and enforce. Jesus came to render this full obedience in His own person, and also to secure that it should be rendered increasingly, and ever increasingly, in the persons of His disciples, the subjects of His kingdom. It is this latter idea that was prominently in His mind on the present occasion, as is evident from the 19th and 20th verses. He came, not to introduce licence and licentiousness into His kingdom, but to establish holiness. Some expositors suppose that the word fulfil means to supplement or perfect; and they imagine that Christ is here referring to His legislative authority. But such an interpretation of the term is at variance with verses 18 and 19, and with its use in kindred passages, such as Rom. 13:, Gal. 5:14. Theophylact, among other interpretations, says that Christ fulfilled the law as a painter fills up the sketch of his picture. But it is a different full filling that is referred to. When commandments are addressed to us, they present, as it were, empty vessels of duty, which our obedience is to fill full."* [19]

---

[19] James Morrison, *A Practical Commentary on the Gospel According to St. Matthew* (London: Hodder & Stoughton, 1895), 67-68.

Howard Crosby — Verse 18: *"One jot or one tittle. Jot is the letter 'Jod,' the smallest letter of the Hebrew alphabet. A tittle (or rather the Greek word thus translated), is a letter-mark distinguishing one letter from another and is thus smaller even than a jot. This is an Oriental way of affirming the complete truthfulness of the Old Testament Scriptures."* [20]

Philip Schaff — Verse 19: *"An application of the truth just announced. —Whosoever, therefore, because of this permanent character of the law. — Shall break, or at any time may break, one of these least commandments, the smallest part of this law, or, in the wider sense, of this revelation which God has made, and shall teach men so, by example or precept, shall be called, recognized as, least in the kingdom of heaven, in the new dispensation He was proclaiming. Such are not excluded, because not opposing the law as a whole, but only some of its minutiae. 'Least' may allude to the Jewish distinction between great and small commandments, a distinction revived by the Romanists, but which cannot exist in God's law. The positive declaration which follows corresponds. The subsequent part of the chapter, especially the next verse, shows that our Lord does not command a strict observance of the letter of the ceremonial law. He there condemns those most scrupulous on these points. The fulfilment and the keeping of the law here required are explained by the fuller light shed upon it by the Saviour's exposition. — He shall be called great. 'He' is emphatic here."* [21]

Simon Patrick — Verse 20: *"For I say unto you, Except your righteousness exceed the righteousness of the scribes and pharisees. Except (1.) you observe all the precepts of the moral law, not making any of them void by your traditions, not leaving undone the 'more weighty matters of the law, judgment, mercy, and faith,' as they do (Matt, 23:23), not*

---

[20] Howard Crosby, *The New Testament, With Brief Explanatory Notes or Scholia* (New York: Charles Scribner, 1863) 10.

[21] Philip Shaff, *A Popular Commentary on the New Testament, Volume 1* (New York: Charles Scribner's Sons, 1891), 60.

 *thinking to atone for the neglect of some of them by your observance of the rest: see notes on James 2:10. (2.) Unless you do observe this law, not only according to the outward man and in the letter, but also in the spiritual sense, and so as to cleanse your hearts from those inward dispositions which are in God's sight violations of it, and 'defile the man,' you will not be fitted to enter into my kingdom. And that in both these things the legal righteousness of the scribes and pharisees was deficient, is clear, (1.) from our Saviour's care to teach them, it was not sufficient to observe what was said to them of old, according to the letter only, but that they were to regard the higher and spiritual sense of it, not only not to 'kill, but not to be angry without cause,' (2.) that adultery might be committed in the heart as well as in the outward action (ver. 28), and that 'what cometh out of the heart defileth the man:' which doctrine the pharisees were so unacquainted with, that they were offended at it (Matt. 25:12). And Josephus, who was well acquainted with their doctrine, declares Polybius mistaken, when he saith Antiochus Epiphanes perished because he would have robbed Diana's temple of its treasure; for, saith, 'He deserveth no punishment for what he only would have done, but did not.' And Kimchi, on these words of David (Ps. 66:18), 'If I regard iniquity in my heart, the Lord will not hear me,' comments thus, 'He will not impute it to me for sin; for God does not look upon an evil thought as sin, unless it be conceived against God or religion.'"* [22]

---

[22] Simon Patrick, *Critical Commentary and Paraphrase on the Old and New Testament and the Apocrypha, Volume 4 (Gospels to Epistles)* (Philadelphia: Carey & Hart, 1845), 58.

Personal Relationship — Murder
Here Christ Teaches That Murder is Simply the Manifestation of What is Taking Place in the Heart Not Just the Act of Physical Murder.
Matthew 5:21-26

George Whitefield Clark —Verse 21: *"Ye have heard. In the public reading and exposition of the law by the scribes. That it was said by them of old time. Correctly translated, 'to those of old,' or 'to the ancients.' Jesus is referring to the stress put upon the mere letter of the law by the scribes. They taught that this was the full meaning of the law, as given to the ancient people of God, and as confirmed by tradition. Christ is not speaking in opposition to Moses, or to the Old Testament, but to the false exposition of the Pharisees. Going beyond the mere letter, he shows the spirituality and the depth of the law, which in its application reaches the mind and the heart. Compare Paul's experience, Rom. 7:7-12.*

Thou shalt not kill. Ex. 20:13. Jesus begins with the second table of the law concerning duties to our neighbor; and with the Law of Murder, a most obvious precept.

The relation of man to man is more easily apprehended than that of man to God. And if men fail to come up to the requirements of the law in regard to their neighbor, much more would they be likely to fail to meet those higher requirements in regard to God. Indeed, failure in the former would be proof of failure in the latter, 1 John 4:20. And whosoever shall kill, etc. This was added by the traditions of the scribes, limiting the law to actual murder — the outward act — and making it merely an external legal enactment. Danger of the judgment. An inferior court among the Jews; constituted in every city, in conformity with Deut. 16:18, consisting, according to Josephus, of seven persons, and having the power of slaying with the sword. Joseph." [23]

---

[23] George W. Clark, *Clark's Peoples Commentary: The Gospel of Matthew, Volume 1* (Philadelphia: American Baptist Publication Society, 1896), 73-74.

Philip Doddridge —Verse 22: *"But I say unto you, That it was the design of God in this precept to prohibit extravagant passions and abusive language, as well as the most fatal effects of them in destroying the lives of each other: so that whosoever shall, without just cause, be angry with his brother, so as secretly to wish him evil, shall be obnoxious to the judgment, or shall be liable to a worse punishment from God than any that your common courts of judicature can inflict and whosoever to his secret anger shall add opprobrious and contemptuous words; or, for instance, shall say to his brother, Raca, that is, Thou worthless empty fellow, shall be exposed to yet more terrible effects of the Divine resentment, and be obnoxious to a yet severer punishment, that will as far exceed the former as that inflicted by the Sanhedrim, which extends to stoning, does that which follows on the judgment of the inferior courts, which only have the power of the sword, but whosoever, in his unreasonable passion, shall presume to say unto his brother, Thou fool, that is, Thou graceless wicked villain, thereby impeaching his moral character, as well as reflecting on his intellectual, shall be obnoxious to the fire of hell, or to a future punishment more dreadful even than that of being burnt alive in the valley of Hinnom, from whence you borrow the name of those infernal regions."* [24]

Charles John Ellicott —Verses 23-24: *"If thou bring thy gift to the altar. — Literally, if thou shouldst be offering. Our Lord was speaking to Jews as such, and paints, therefore, as it were, a scene in the Jewish Temple. The worshipper is about to offer a 'gift' (the most generic term seems intentionally used to represent any kind of offering) and stands at the altar with the priest waiting to do his work. That is the right time for recollection and self-scrutiny. The worshipper is to ask himself, not whether he has a ground of complaint against anyone, but whether any one has cause of complaint*

---

[24] Philip Doddridge, *The Works of the Rev. P. Doddridge*, Volume 6 (Leeds: Edward Barnes, 1804), 214-207-208.

against him. This, and not the other, is the right question at such a moment — has he injured his neighbour by act, or spoken bitter words of him?

Leave there thy gift. — The words describe an act which would appear to men as a breach of liturgical propriety. To leave the gift and the priest, the act of sacrifice unfinished, would be strange and startling, yet that, our Lord teaches, were better than to sacrifice with the sense of a wrong unconfessed and unatoned for, and, a fortiori, better than the deeper evil of not being ready to forgive. The Talmud gives a curious rule, to which the words may perhaps allude: 'If a man is on the point of offering the Passover, and remembers that there is any leaven left in the house, let him return to his house, and remove it, and then come and finish the Passover' (Pesachim, f. 49). What the scribes laid down as a duty in regard to the 'leaven of bread,' our Lord applies to the leaven of malice and wickedness.

Be reconciled. — It is not enough to see in this only a command to remove ill-will and enmity from our own mind, though that, of course, is implied. There must be also confession of wrong and the endeavour to make amends, to bring about, as far as in us lies, reconciliation, or at-one-ment." [25]

John Bird Sumner —Verses 25-26: *"Agree with thine adversary quickly, whiles thou art in the way with him; lest at any time the adversary deliver thee to the judge, and the judge deliver thee to the officer, and thou be cast into prison. Verily I say unto thee, Thou shalt by no means come out thence, till thou hast paid the uttermost farthing.*

The only way of subduing the evil passions of envy, hatred, and malice, is to repress every hostile feeling in the first bud. Even acts of religious duty, however needful, are not so urgent as this; and till this is done, are displeasing rather than acceptable to God. It was an act of duty to bring a gift to the altar; Moses had commanded,

---

[25] Charles John Ellicott, *A New Testament Commentary for English Readers (Matthew-John), Volume 1* (Edinburg: The Calvin Translation Society, 1884), 26.

(Deut. 16:16.) 'Three times in a year shall all thy males appear before the Lord thy God in the place which he shall choose; in the feast of unleavened bread, and in the feast of weeks, and in the feast of tabernacles: and they shall not appear before the Lord empty; every man shall give as he is able, according to the blessing of the Lord thy God which he hath given thee.' This, then, was an appointed, acknowledged duty. But ill-will rankling at the heart would corrupt all: 'for if a man love not his brother whom he hath seen, how can he love God whom he hath not seen?' How can he entertain that humble, lowly spirit which a befits a sinner in the presence of his Judge, a creature in the worship of his Creator, while towards his brethren on earth he cherishes a malicious, unrelenting disposition?

What then is to done? Must the feeling remain, and excuse the neglect of God? as is sometimes implied, in the reasons which men plead for absenting themselves from the Church, or from the Lord's Table? The way of duty is very different. First be reconciled to thy brother, and then come and offer thy gift. But be reconciled without delay; common worldly prudence requires you to agree with an adversary quickly; we know the consequences which often follow obstinate and persevering hostility even in this world; it often involves men in difficulties from which they endeavour to extricate themselves in vain. How much more serious is delay, when every day, during which you cherish an unforgiving temper, increases your condemnation before God? If thou fallest within the verge of his wrath, how shalt thou escape? Thou hast nothing at all to pay, and yet the uttermost farthing shall be required. If man is our adversary, prudence warns us to seek a timely reconciliation. Let this remind us how dreadful it would be to remain with God for our adversary. 'Seek ye the Lord while he may be found, call ye upon him while he is near.'" [26]

---

[26] John Bird Sumner, *A Practical Exposition of the Gospels of St. Matthew and St. Mark, in the Form of Lectures* (London: Hatchard & Son, 1831), 51-52.

Personal Relationship — Adultery
Make Note Our Savior Clearly Teaches We Can Commit Adultery in the Mind as Well as by the Literal Act.
Matthew 5:27-30

Albert Barnes —Verses 27-30: *"Ye have heard thou shalt not commit adultery. Our Saviour in these verses explains the seventh commandment. It is probable that the Pharisees had explained this commandment as they had the sixth, as extending only to the external act; and that they regarded evil thoughts and a wanton imagination as of little consequence, or as not forbidden by the law. Our Saviour assures them that the commandment did not regard the external act merely, but the secrets of the heart, and the movements of the eye. That they who indulged a wanton desire; that they who looked on a woman to increase their lust, have already, in the sight of God, violated the commandment, and committed adultery in the heart. Such was the guilt of David, whose deep and awful crime fully shows the danger of indulging in evil desires, and in the rovings of a wanton eye. See 2 Sam. 11, Ps. 51. See also 2 Pet. 2:14. So exceeding strict and broad is the law of God! And so heinous in his sight are thoughts and feelings, which may be forever concealed from the world.*

Thy right eye. The Hebrews, like others, were accustomed to represent the affections of the mind by the members or parts of the body. Rom. 7:23; 6:13. Thus the bowels, denoted compassion; the heart, affection or feeling; the reins, understanding, secret purpose. An evil eye denotes sometimes envy (Matt. 20:15.); sometimes an evil passion, or sin in general. Mark 7:21, 22. — 'Out of the heart proceedeth an evil eye.' In this place, as in 2 Peter 2:14, it is used to denote strong adulterous passion, unlawful desire, and inclination. The right eye and hand are mentioned, because they are of most use to us, and denote that, however strong the passion may be, or difficult to part with, yet that we should do it. Shall offend thee. The noun from which the verb 'offend,'

in the original, is derived, commonly means a stumbling-block, or a stone placed in the way, over which one might fall. It also means a net, or a certain part of a net against which, if a bird strikes, it springs the net, and is taken. It comes to signify, therefore, anything by which we fall, or are ensnared; and applied to morals, means anything by which we fall into sin, or by which we are ensnared. The English word offend means now, commonly, to displease; to make angry; to affront. This is by no means the sense of the word in scripture. It means to cause to fall, or to allure, into sin. The eye does this, when it wantonly looks on a woman to lust after her. Pluck it out. It cannot be supposed that Christ intended this to be taken literally. His design was to teach that the dearest objects, if they caused us to sin, were to be abandoned; that by all sacrifices and self-denials, we must overcome the evil propensities of our natures, and resist our wanton imaginations. Some of the Fathers, however, took this commandment literally. Our Saviour several times repeated this sentiment. See Matt, 15:9. Mark 9:43—47. See also Col. 3:5. It is profitable for thee. It is better for thee. You will be a gainer by it. One of thy members perish. It is better to deny yourself the gratification of an evil passion here, however much it may cost you, than to go down to hell for ever. Thy whole body be cast into hell. Thy body with all its unsubdued and vicious propensities. This will constitute no small part of the misery of hell. The sinner will be sent there as he is, with every evil desire; every unsubdued propensity; every wicked and troublesome passion; and yet with no possibility of gratification. It constitutes our highest notions of misery, when we think of a man filled with anger, pride, malice, avarice, envy, and lust, and no opportunity of gratifying them forever. This is all that is necessary to make an eternal hell." [27]

---

[27] Albert Barnes, *Explanatory and Practical, on the Gospels Designed for Sunday School Teachers and Bible Classes, Volume 1* (Philadelphia: Harper & Brothers, 1840), 71-72.

Personal Relationship — Divorce
Jesus Contrast the Current Religious Understanding of Following the Law With His Understanding of It.
Matthew 5:31-32

David Brown —Verses 31-32: *"It hath been said. This shortened form was perhaps intentional, to mark a transition from the commandments of the Decalogue to a civil enactment on the subject of Divorce, quoted from Deut. 14:1. The law of Divorce — according to its strictness or laxity — has so intimate a bearing upon purity in the married life, that nothing could be more natural than to pass from the seventh commandment to the loose views on that subject then current. Whosoever shall put away his wife, let him give her a writing of divorcement — a legal check upon reckless and Tyrannical separation. The one legitimate ground of divorce allowed by the enactment just quoted was 'some uncleanness'—in other words, conjugal infidelity. But while one school of interpreters (that of Shammai) explained this quite correctly, as prohibiting divorce in every case save that of adultery, another school (that of Hillel) stretched the expression so far as to include everything in the wife offensive or disagreeable to the husband—a view of the law too well fitted to minister to caprice and depraved inclination not to find extensive favour. And, indeed, to this day the Jews allow divorces on the most frivolous pretexts. It was to meet this that our Lord uttered what follows: 32. But I say unto you, That whosoever shall put away his wife, saving for the cause of fornication, causeth her to commit adultery — that is, drives her into it, in case she marries again; and whosoever shall marry her that is divorced — for anything short of conjugal infidelity, committeth adultery — for if the commandment is broken by the one party, it must be by the other also. But see on chap. 19:4-9. Whether the innocent party, after a just divorce, may lawfully marry again, is not treated of here. The Church of Rome says, No; but the Greek and Protestant Churches allow it.* [28]

---

[28] Robert Jamieson, A. R. Fausett, David Brown, *A Commentary, Critical, Experimental, and Practical, on the Old and New Testaments, Volume 5 (Matthew-John by David Brown)* (Philadelphia: L. P. Lippincott, 1866), 34.

An Ordinary Commentary by Ordinary Men: The Sermon on the Mount

Personal Relationship — Oaths
Jesus Teaches the Foolishness of Mans Flippant and Hypocritical Oaths We Use in Order to Make an Impression on Others.
Matthew 5:33-37

Charles Rosenbury Erdman —Verses 33-37: *"33 Again, ye have heard that it was said to them of old time, Thou shalt not forswear thyself, but shalt perform unto the Lord thine oaths: 34 but I say unto you, Swear not at all; neither by the heaven, for it is the throne of God; 35 nor by the earth, for it is the footstool of his feet; nor by Jerusalem, for it is the city of the great King. 36 Neither shalt thou swear by thy head, for thou canst not make one hair white*  *or black. 37 But let your speech be, Yea, yea; Nay, nay: and whatsoever is more than these is of the evil one.*

The next example of the true interpretation of the moral law refers to the requirements both of the Third and the Ninth Commandments. It warns against both profanity and unfaithfulness to promises. It does not refer to oaths taken in courts of law. These safeguard and secure the truth which is regarded as sacred and is fully protected by the very interpretation of the law upon which Jesus here insists. The Pharisee, at least the formalist, regarded himself as bound by an oath provided it was stated in certain words. To his mind the slightest verbal change relieved him from all moral obligation. Then again he excused himself for his profanity in case he did not mention some special form of the divine name. He believed he could swear by the throne of God, or by the earth, or by Jerusalem; but Jesus suggests that all these are contrary to the Commandment which forbids us to take the name of the Lord in vain. He insists that our speech should be simple; that our language should be purged of extravagance; that our purposes, our thoughts, and our lives should be so sincere and so pure and so honest, that a simple 'yes' or 'no' in our social intercourse, and in our usual dealings with others should quite suffice to satisfy them of the truthfulness of our statements." [29]

---

[29] Charles R. Erdman, *The Gospel of Matthew: An Exposition* (Philadelphia: The Westminister Press, 1920), 51.

Personal Relationship — Eye for an Eye

It Has Always been a False Notion and Teaching That a Person Has The Right to Justify or Believe They May License Themselves to Inflict Revenge or Retaliation on Others.
Matthew 5:38-42

David Thomas —Verse 38: "*Revenge is another evil here referred to. Ye have heard that it hath been said, an 'eye for an eye, and a tooth for a tooth:' The principle of jus talionis, which has been acted upon by the Jews, had also become the common dictate of humanity. To return evil for evil was a general practice, which was even regarded as justifiable. Jesus here proscribes it. When he says, 'resist not evil' He does not mean that we are not to defend ourselves when threatened with danger. The principle of self-defence is innate, and an innate principle is divine; and divine principles Christ came not 'to destroy, but to fulfil.' He means that we are never to do it in a spirit of revenge. It is revenge which He proscribes, and revenge is another of the primary evils of the world. It is an all-consuming fire in the soul. It burns up all kindly feelings of our nature. The man under its influence has no mercy on himself, and may truly say, the pains of hell have got hold upon me.* [30]

Henry Thornton —Verse 39: "'*But I say unto you,' says He, 'that ye resist not evil; but whosoever shall smite thee on thy right cheek, turn to him the other also.' Certainly, expressions of this kind are not to be taken literally: but let us beware of an altogether loose interpretation. Let us not in this respect imitate the Pharisees. They interpreted the Old Testament in such a manner as to favour their own corrupt prejudices: let us not bend the New to our crooked and imperfect practice.*

---

[30] David Thomas, *The Genius of the Gospel: A Homiletical Commentary on the Gospel of St. Matthew* (London: Dickinson & Higham, 1873), 46-47.

The meaning of all those strong expressions of our Saviour, which we are now considering, may be thus explained. It is, as if He had said, 'Think not because the law hath declared, an eye for an eye, and a tooth for a tooth, that it will justify that spirit of private resentment and retaliation which it is made to do. Such indeed is the perverse turn given to it by your Scribes and Pharisees. But I am come to prescribe to you a far higher rule of duty. I teach that a man not only must not resent injuries, and demand reparation to the utmost, but must learn patiently to endure injuries, and to forbear from any revenge whatever. 'I say unto You that ye resist not evil.' There must be such a spirit in my followers, that however great may be the ill-treatment which they receive, they must be willing quietly to suffer it; as much so as if, when a man were to smite thee on the right cheek, thou wert to turn to him the other also. Revenge is utterly excluded out of my code. The law of My Kingdom is that of the free forgiveness of each other." [31]

William McIntyre —Verse 40: *"If any man will sue thee at the law. — The case put must be one of wrong, for otherwise there would be no room for retaliation; and the wrong supposed is, that someone unrighteously lays claims to your coat, and intends to take the law of you with the view of enforcing his claim. Conduct so iniquitous and disgraceful would be peculiarly calculated to provoke retaliation; but our Lord requires that, rather than retaliate or repel the unjust demand in a vindictive, retaliating spirit, you not only at once give your coat to the unrighteous claimant, but 'let him have your cloak also.' He does not absolutely require that you pursue this course; he only requires that you pursue it rather than act on the traditional maxim of 'an eye for an eye, and a tooth for a tooth.' What you have to do is to avoid retaliation, and if, for the purpose of*

---

[31] Henry Thornton, *Family Prayers, and Prayers on the Ten Commandments, to Which Added A Commentary of the Sermon Upon the Mount* (New York: Stanford & Swords, 1846), 243-244.

avoiding it, you must part with your coat, then by all means part with it, and with your cloak also if that be necessary. The 'coat' or tunic was an inner garment made of cotton or linen, and the 'cloak' was a loose outer garment, and, as being larger and often of more costly materials, was of greater value than the tunic." [32]

Lyman Abbott —Verse 41: *"41. Whosoever shall compel thee to go, etc. The word translated compel is of Persian origin. Footmen were employed from a very early period of history in carrying despatches (1 Sam. 22:17; 2 Chron. 30:6, 10). At a later period, this service was performed with mules and camels (Esther 3:13, with 15; 8:10, 14). It was continued under the Roman government, and these heralds were authorized to compel any person to accompany them as guides or assistants, or to lend them a horse, boat, or other means of transportation. A similar law is in force in Persia to this day. The Jews particularly objected to the duty thus imposed on them. Christ's disciples were to yield to the demand, though oppressive and injurious."* [33]

John Guyse —Verse 42: *"And that you may, as much as possible, promote the welfare of others, be ready, according to your ability, to relieve the necessities of such as apply to you for help; and if they desire you to lend them anything that they greatly want the use of, do not deny them, in case you can let them have it without the hazard of a loss too great for your own circumstances to bear; or if you cannot conveniently grant their request, yet deal tenderly with them, and do not turn away in a huff."* [34]

---

[32] William McIntyre, *Exposition of the Sermon on the Mount, Matthew 5-7* (Edinburgh: Johnstone & Hunter, 1854), 166-167.

[33] Lyman Abbott, 1876, *The New Testament with Notes and Comments: Accompanied with Maps and Illustrations (Matthew and Mark)* (New York: A. S. Barnes & Company, 1876) 95.

[34] John Guyse, *The Practical Expositor or An Exposition of the New Testament, in the Form of a Paraphrase, Volume 1* (Edinburgh: Ogle, Allardice & Thomson, 1818), 32.

Personal Relationship — Love Your Enemies

Nowhere In God's Word Are We Taught or Instructed To Hate Our Enemies — No Where! In Fact it is One of the Highest Acts of Affection That Glorifies God.

Matthew 5:43-48

William Nast — Verse 43: *"Verse 43. Thou shalt love thy neighbor and hate thine enemy. The first clause of this precept is found Lev. 19:18; the second is found nowhere in the Old Testament Scriptures; the false interpretations of the Pharisees culminates here in an arbitrary addition to the law, which mutilates it and completely destroys its meaning. The first step taken in this misinterpretation and perversion was to restrict the precepts of love to the Israelites and the stranger sojourning with them exclusively, (Lev. 19:33, 34;) the second was to make 'not to love' equal to hating. When Moses uses neighbor and fellow-Israelite as apparently synonymous terms, he does so because the Jew, shut up from intercourse with the surrounding Gentiles in so many ways, could ordinarily practice the commandment of love only on his fellow-Jew; but that the two terms are not synonymous, that the law of love includes the Gentile also, is proved by the Decalogue. For who can believe for a moment that the Jew would be guiltless in bearing false witness against the Gentile, or in coveting his wife, etc.? Moreover, the term neighbor is used with reference to the Gentiles before the law was given. (Ex. 11:2; Gen. 38:20.)."* [35]

James Glentworth Butler — Verse 44: *"44. Love your enemies. Love as God loves, regardless of merit and of the reciprocity of love; loving because you would be like God, loving because God has first loved you.— There is nothing greater than to imitate God in doing good to our enemies. If God had not loved us while we were his enemies, we*

---

[35] William Nast, *A Commentary on the Gospels of Matthew and Mark* (Cincinnati: Poe & Hitchcock, 1864), 258-259.

could never have become his children; and we shall cease to be so, if we cease to imitate him. This precept alone is a sufficient proof of the holiness of the gospel, and of the truth of the Christian religion. None but God could have imposed a yoke so contrary to self-love; and nothing but the supreme and infinite love could have made men practise a law so insupportable to corrupt nature. — He who has exhorted and taught us to pardon, is undoubtedly a God who pardons. His anger, all divine, takes nothing from his love. Were he man, he would pray for these enemies of his will? Jesus Christ, his Son, prayed for the enemies of his Father. The more our personal resentment is effaced in the sadness of seeing our Father offended, the weak scandalized, the seeds of sin multiplied, the empire of darkness extended, the more will our heart be free to pardon, to love, and to pray." [36]

William Burkitt —Verse 45: "*That ye may be the children of your Father which is in heaven: for he maketh his sun to rise on the evil and on the good, and sendeth rain on the just and on the unjust.* To encourage us to the foregoing duty of loving our enemies, our Saviour propounds the example of God himself to our imitation, That ye may he the children of your Father; that is, that you may be known to be the children of your Father which is in heaven, by your likeness to him, and imitation of him. Note, 1. That the best evidence we can have of our divine sonship, is our conformity to the divine nature, especially in those excellent properties of goodness and forgiveness. Note, 2. That God doth good to them that are continually doing evil unto him. Rain and sun, fat and sweet, gold and silver, are such good things as their hearts and houses are filled with, who are altogether empty of grace and goodness." [37]

---

[36] J. Glentworth Butler, *The Bible Readers' Commentary: The New Testament*, in Two Volumes, Volume 1 (New York: D. Appleton & Company, 1878), 153-154.

[37] William Burkitt, *Expository Notes, with Practical Observations, on the New Testament of our Lord and Saviour Jesus Christ*, Volume 1 (Philadelphia: Thomas Wardle, 1835), 24.

Thomas Manton —Verse 46: *"'If ye love them that love you, what reward shall ye have? do not even the publicans the same?' The publicans were accounted the most vile and unworthy men in that age; but a publican would love those of his own party; therefore a Christian that is acquainted with Christ's love to strangers, to enemies, should manage his affections with more excellency and pureness. The world is not acquainted with the love of Christ, and therefore only loveth 'its own,' but we are acquainted with it, and therefore should love others. See John 13:34, 'See that ye love one another, as I have loved you.' Jesus Christ came from heaven, not only to repair and preserve the notions of the Godhead by the greatness of his sufferings, but to propound to us a more exact pattern of charity, and to elevate duty between man and man."* [38]

John Heyl Vincent —Verse 47: *"Salute your brethren only — Here, most probably, in its literal sense. Jews did not salute Gentiles. Mohammedans do not salute Christians even now in the East. — Alford. More than others —The Christian may not compare himself with others and be satisfied because he is as others. Both God and men expect more of him than of others, and this in the common intercourse of daily life. — Abbott. The question is suggestive of duty. It implies that Christians ought to do more in this world than others. We may ask, For whom? For themselves, in the way of cultivating a more noble, consistent, and Christ-like character; for their families, in the way of leading them to Christ and training them for God and for heaven; for their immediate neighborhood, their country, and the world, in the way of propagating truth, lessening sorrow, preventing sin, and extending the kingdom of Christ. —J. Morgan."* [39]

---

[38] Thomas Manton, *The Works of Thomas Manton, Volume 5* (London: James Nibet & Company, 1871), 95.

[39] J. H. Vincent, *The Lesson Commentary on the International Lessons for 1880* (London: Elliot Stock, 1879), 54.

John Calvin —Verse 48: *"You shall therefore be perfect. This perfection does not mean equality but relates solely to resemblance. However distant we are from the perfection of God, we are said to be perfect, as he is perfect, when we aim at the same object, which he presents to us in Himself. Should it be thought preferable, we may state it thus. There is no comparison here made between God and us: but the perfection of God means, first, that free and pure kindness, which is not induced by the expectation of gain; and, secondly, that remarkable goodness, which contends with the malice and ingratitude of men. This appears more clearly from the words of Luke, Be ye therefore merciful, as your Father also is merciful: for mercy is contrasted with a mercenary regard, which is founded on private advantage."* [40]

---

[40] John Calvin, *A Commentary On a Harmony of the Evangelists, Matthew, Mark, and Luke, Volume 1* (Edinburg: The Calvin Translation Society, 1836), 308.

Matthew 6

Types of Righteousness and Religion

Our Lord Warns His Followers Against Counterfeit Spirituality Seeking to Be Seen and Praised By Men.
Matthew 6:1-18

Harvey Goodwin —Verse 1: *"In these verses our Lord applies to the subject of almsgiving, to what we commonly call in these days charity, the same spiritual principles according to which He has already explained and expanded several of the Laws of the Old Testament. All the men of our Lord's time would admit almsgiving to the poor to be a great duty; but then many of them held or seemed to hold that there was virtue in the mere giving, independently of the spirit in which it was done, so that a man might make his charitable doings redound to his own praise, sounding a trumpet when he was going to distribute his alms, and the rest. Our Lord declares that, of which we can have no doubt when we hear it asserted, namely, that in the sight of God such almsgiving can have no virtue, no beauty, no excellence: the spirit which can alone render almsgiving pleasing to Him who sees the heart is the simple spirit of love, which withdraws itself from observation, seeks not its own, is unselfish, desiring to do what is charitable for the sake of charity only.*

But mark the awful emphasis, and something like irony, with which our Saviour says of those who make parade of their charity, Verily I say unto you, They have their reward; yes, they have their reward; they wish to gain the attention of mankind, and they gain it; they wish for applause, and they have it; they are pleased when they hear people say, 'What a liberal man he is! and they have plenty of pleasure such as this. But what does it all amount to? What treasure is laid up in heaven by mere earthly applause? What satisfaction can it be to have cheated men into the belief of our excellent qualities, if the rottenness of our hearts is open and undisguised in the sight of Him who sees in secret, and who knows the thoughts and intents of the heart? They have their reward, have it already in this present world, and a poor unsatisfactory delusive reward it is." [41]

Charles Haddon Spurgeon —Verses 2-4: *"Therefore when thou doest thine alms, do not sound a trumpet before thee, as the hypocrites do in the synagogues and in the streets, that they may have glory of men. Verily I say unto you, they have their reward.* We must not copy the loud charity of certain vainglorious persons: their character is hypocritical, their manner is ostentatious, their aim is to be seen of men, their reward is in the present. That reward is a very poor one and is soon over. To stand with a penny in one hand and a trumpet in the other is the posture of hypocrisy. 'Glory of men' is a thing which can be bought: but honour from God is a very different thing. This is an advertising age, and too many are saying, 'Behold my liberality!" Those who have Jesus for their King must wear his livery of humility, and not the scarlet trappings of a purse-proud generosity, which blows its own trumpet, not only in the streets, but even in the synagogues. We cannot expect two rewards for the same action: if we have it now, we shall not have it hereafter. Unrewarded alms will alone count in the record of the last day.

But when thou doest alms, let not thy left hand know what thy right hand doeth: that thine atms may be in secret: and thy Father which seeth in secret himself shalt reward thee openly. Seek secrecy for your good deeds. Do not even see your own virtue. Hide from yourself that which you yourself have done that is commendable; for the proud contemplation of your own generosity may tarnish all your alms. Keep the thing so secret that even you yourself are hardly aware that you are doing anything at all praiseworthy. Let God be present, and you will have enough of an audience. He will reward you, reward you 'openly,' reward you as a Father rewards a child, reward you as one who saw what you did, and knew that you did it wholly unto him.

[41] Harvey Goodwin, *A Commentary on the Gospel of S. Matthew* (Cambridge: Deighton, Bell and Company, 1857), 93-94.

Lord, help me, when I am doing good, to keep my left hand out of it, that I may have no sinister motive, and no desire to have a present reward of praise among my fellow-men." [42]

William Nast —Verse 5: *"The Jews attached to prayer a still greater importance than even to fasting and almsgiving but had reduced it to a mere mechanical performance. They prayed three times a day, at nine o'clock, A.M., at twelve o'clock, and at three o'clock, P. M., and resorted to the synagogue for prayer on the Sabbath, on Monday, and Thursday. Many a zealous Jew spent nine hours a day in prayer. Nor did they go for public prayer only to*  *the synagogue, but, like the Roman Catholics, also for private prayer, because greater efficacy was ascribed to prayer in the synagogue. The Pharisees managed it so — this is implied in 'they love' — that they were overtaken by the hour of prayer while on their way to the synagogue, that the people might see them pray and praise their piety. It is evident from the context that these remarks of our Lord are not directed against common or public prayer — a duty resting on express Divine command — but against performing private prayer in public places."* [43]

Adam Clarke —Verse 6: *"But thou, when thou prayest. This is a very impressive and emphatic address. But thou! whosoever thou art, Jew, Pharisee, Christian — enter into thy closet. Prayer is the most secret intercourse of the soul with God, and as it were the conversation of one heart with another. The world is too profane and treacherous to be of the secret. We must shut the door against it: endeavour to forget it, with all the affairs which busy and*  *amuse it. Prayer requires retirement, at least of the heart; for this may be fitly termed the closet in the house of God, which house the body of every real Christian is, 1 Cor. 3:16. To this closet we ought to retire even in public prayer, and in the midst of company.*

[42] Charles H. Spurgeon, *The Gospel of the Kingdom: A Popular Exposition of the Gospel According to Matthew* (London: Passmore & Alabaster, 1893), 32.

[43] William Nast, *A Commentary on the Gospels of Matthew and Mark* (Cincinnati: Poe & Hitchcock, 1864), 262.

Reward thee openly. What goodness is there equal to this of God! to give, not only what we ask, and more than we ask, but to reward even prayer itself! How great advantage is it to serve a prince who places prayers in the number of services, and reckons to his subjects' account, even their trust and confidence in begging all things of him!" [44]

James Morison —Verse 7: *"But, in addition to secrecy as regards men, take heed as regards another matter, namely, the fitting mood of mind in relation to God, when engaged in praying, use not vain repetitions: 'Battering' away at God, as it were, and 'blattering.' 'Babble' not in prayer, in the spirit of those worshippers of Baal 'who called on his name from morning even until noon, saying, O Baal, hear us' (1 Kings 18:26), or of those worshippers of Diana who 'about the space of two hours cried out, Great is Diana of the Ephesians' (Acts 19:34). As the Gentiles do; for they think that they shall be heard for their much speaking: They think that in heaping word upon word, and persistently holding on with their speechifying, they shall secure attention and a hearing. Such multiplication of speaking is utterly in vain. 'It proceedeth,' as good David Dickson remarks, 'from a base misconception of God.' It is well observed however by Augustin that there is a great difference between much speaking and much praying. And even repetitiousness, when it is not wordiness but the expression of intensity of desire, will not be unacceptable to the Hearer of prayer. Such repetitiousness will not be immoderate. It is found in many of the psalms; and it was characteristic of our Saviors' own prayer in the garden of Gethsemane, when He again and again 'prayed, saying the same words' (Matt. 26:44)."* [45]

James Glentworth Butler —Verse 8: *"Your Father knoweth what ye need. Prayer is the preparation and the enlargement of the heart for the receiving of the divine gift; which, indeed, God is always prepared to give, but we are not always prepared to receive. In the act of prayer*

---

[44] Adam Clarke, *The New Testament of Our Lord Jesus Christ (Matthew to the Acts), Volume 1* (New York: Lane & Scott, 1850), 84.
[45] James Morrison, *A Practical Commentary on the Gospel According to St. Matthew* (London: Hodder & Stoughton, 1895), 88.

there is a purging of the spiritual eye, which thus is averted from the things earthly that darken it, and becomes receptive of the divine light — able not to endure only the brightness of that light, but to rejoice in it with an ineffable joy. In the earnest asking is the enlargement of the heart for the abundant receiving; even as in it is also the needful preparation for the receiving with a due thankfulness; while, on the contrary, the good which came unsought would too often remain the unacknowledged also. Prayer is not designed to inform God, but to give man a sight of his misery, to humble his heart, to excite his desire, to inflame his faith, to animate his hope, to raise his soul toward heaven, and to put him in mind that there is his Father, his country, his inheritance. He is a Father to whom we pray; let us go to him with confidence; he knows our wants; let us remove far from us all anxious disquiet and concern."* [46]

Edwin Wilbur Rice —Verse 9: *"After this manner, or 'thus.' Jesus gives a pattern or specimen of true prayer. Thus it was understood by nearly all the early fathers and by the majority of evangelical Christians. Some hold that he gave this as a formula always to be used. Others say this is against his teaching in v. 7; and that he did not make the use of this particular form obligatory on his followers. There is no historical evidence, so far as known, that it was used as a formula of prayer by the apostles themselves. It is to be accepted as a proper mode of prayer, and it may be used in the worship of God privately or publicly, but always and only in accord with the principle already declared by Jesus — not to use display or vain repetitions in praying.*

Our Father. 'The Lord's Prayer,' so called because the Lord gave it as a pattern, might more accurately be called 'The Model Prayer.' It is usually divided into three parts: 1, preface; 2, petitions.; 3, conclusion. The Latin fathers and the Lutheran Church make the number of the

---

[46] J. Glentworth Butler, *The Bible Work (or Bible Readers Commentary) The New Testament, in Two Volumes, Volume 1* (New York: Funk & Wagnalls, 1889), 157.

petitions seven. The Greek and Reformed Churches and the Westminster divines make the number six, by making only one petition of the first part of v. 13, while the others divide it into two petitions. The works written on this 'Model Prayer' would make an immense library. The Preface is literally 'Father of us, who art in the heavens;' 'our,' not my, implying the brotherhood of the human race, especially of believers. The 'fatherhood of God' was an old thought in the Jewish worship. It seems a common thought of the race. The Vedas of India, the Zend-Avesta of Persia, Greek literature, as Plato and Plutarch, and the older Baal worship, have the same idea. It seems to be a relic of God's earliest revelation of himself in patriarchal times. But Jesus brings it into a new form and touches it with a new life.

First Petition. Hallowed be thy name. That is, help us and others to revere, hallow, sanctify and make holy God's name and being. Reverence lies at the foundation of all true prayer. [47]

Philip Schaff —Verse 10: *"Thy kingdom come (second petition). The Messiah's kingdom, which in organized form had not yet come, but was proclaimed by the Lord Himself, as at hand. It did speedily come, as opposed to the Old Testament theocracy; but in its fulness, including the triumph of Christ's kingdom over the kingdom of darkness it has not yet come. For this coming we now pray, and the prayer is answered, in part by every success of the gospel, and will be answered entirely when the King comes again. A missionary petition, but not less a prayer for our own higher sanctification and for the second coming of Christ. —Thy will be done as in heaven, so on earth (Third petition). 'Heaven' and 'earth,' put for their inhabitants. As by pure angels, so by men. The idea of human doing is prominent, our will subordinate to God's will. 'As' expresses similarity in kind and completeness."* [48]

---

[47] Edwin W. Rice, *Commentary on the Gospel According to Matthew* (Philadelphia: The American Sunday School Union, 1897), 79.

[48] Philip Schaff, *A Popular Commentary on the New Testament, Volume 1* (New York: Charles Scribner's Sons, 1891), 67.

Matthew Henry —Verse 11: *"Give us this day our daily bread. Because our natural being is necessary to our spiritual well-being in this world, therefore, after the things of God's glory, kingdom, and will, we pray for the necessary supports and comforts of this present life, which are the gifts of God, and must be asked of him, — Bread for the day approaching, for all the remainder of our lives. Bread for the time to come, or bread for our being and subsistence, that which is agreeable to our condition in the world, (Prov. 30:8.) food convenient for us and our families, according to our rank and station.*

Every word here has a lesson in it: (1.) We ask for bread; that teaches us sobriety and temperance; we ask for bread, not dainties, not superfluities; that which is wholesome, though it be not nice. (2.) We ask for our bread; that teaches us honesty and industry: we do not ask for the bread out of other people's mouths, not the bread of deceit, (Prov. 20:13.) not the bread of idleness, (Prov. 31:27.) but the bread honestly gotten. (3.) We ask for our daily bread; which teaches us not to take thought for the morrow, (Ch. 6:34.) but constantly to depend upon divine providence, as those that live from hand to mouth. (4.) We beg of God to give it us, not sell it us, nor lend it us, but give it. The greatest of men must be beholden to the mercy of God for their daily bread. (5.) We pray, 'Give it to us; not to me only, but to others in common with me.' This teaches us charity, and a compassionate concern for the poor and needy. It intimates also, that we ought to pray with our families; we and our households eat together, and therefore ought to pray together. (6.) We pray that God would give it us this day; which teaches us to renew the desire of our souls toward God, as the wants of our bodies are renewed; as duly as the day comes, we must pray to our heavenly Father, and reckon we should as well go a day without meat, as without prayer." [49]

John Bird Sumner —Verses 12-13: *"And forgive us our trespasses, as we forgive them that trespass against us. We are, then, trespassers: we need forgiveness. Our hearts must be ill-instructed in the divine law,*

---

[49] Matthew Henry, *An Exposition of the Old and New Testament*, Volume 5 (Philadelphia: Edward Barrington & George D. Haswell, 1825), 67.

if they do not tell us that it is so. And he who lives through mercy, must show mercy. An unforgiving spirit would mar the effect even of this Christian prayer, because it would betray a most unchristian state of mind.

And lead us not into temptation but deliver us from evil. There are temptations which 'are common to men.' We see throughout all Scripture, that it is God's will that his people should be tried. But who, that knows his frailty, and the infirmity of his best purposes, will not pray that he may be kept from temptation, and delivered from the evil one?"[50]

Joseph Addison Alexander —Verses 14-15: "*For, if ye forgive men their trespasses, your heavenly Father will also forgive you. But, if ye forgive not men their trespasses, neither will your Father forgive your trespasses.* The next two verses, as already stated, purport to give a reason for something in the previous context, which can only be the last clause of v. 12. As if he had said, 'In asking for forgiveness, you must stand prepared to exercise it also, for unless you are, you cannot be forgiven, not because the one is the condition of the other, but because the two must go together, and the absence of the one proves the absence of the other.' The verb four times repeated here is the same with that in v. 12; but instead of the word delts another figure is employed, that of a fall or false step, rendered in the English versions, trespass, and intended to express the same idea, that of sin, which may be considered either as a debt due to the divine justice, or as a lapse from the straight course of moral rectitude. The fulness and precision with which the alternative is here presented may appear superfluous, but adds to the solemnity of the assurance, and would no doubt strengthen the impression on the minds of the original hearers. In this, as in the whole preceding context, God is still presented in his fatherly relation to all true believers; as if to in-

---

[50] John Bird Sumner, *A Practical Exposition of the Gospels of St. Matthew and St. Mark, in the Form of Lectures* (London: Hatchard & Son, 1831), 70.

timate that even that relation, tender as it is, would give no indulgence to an unforgiving spirit." [51]

Charles John Elliott —Verse 16: *"When ye fast. — Fasting had risen under the teaching of the Pharisees into a new prominence. Under the Law there had been but the one great fast of the Day of Atonement, on which men were 'to afflict their souls' (Lev. 23:27; Num. 24:7), and practice had interpreted that phrase as meaning total abstinence from food. Other fasts were occasional, in times of distress or penitence, as in Joel 1:14, 2:15; or as part of a policy*  *affecting to be religions zeal (1 Kings 21:9, 12); or as the expression of personal sorrow (1 Sam. 20:34; 2 Sam. 12:16; Ezra 10:6; Neh. 1:4; et al.). These were observed with an ostentatious show of affliction which called forth the indignant sarcasm of the prophets (Isa. 58:5). The 'sackcloth' took the place of the usual raiment, 'ashes' on the head, of the usual unguents (Neh. 9:1; Ps.35:13). The tradition of the Pharisees, starting from the true principle that fasting was one way of attaining self-control, and that as a discipline it was effectual in proportion as it was systematic, fixed on the fasts 'twice in the week,' specified in the prayer of the Pharisee (Luke 18:12); and the second and fifth days of the week were fixed, and connected with some vague idea that Moses went up Mount Sinai on the one, and descended on the other. Our Lord, we may note, does not blame the principle, or even the rule, on which the Pharisees acted. He recognises fasting, as He recognises almsgiving and prayer, and is content to warn His disciples against the ostentation that vitiates all three, the secret self-satisfaction under the mask of contrition, the 'pride that apes humility.' The very words, 'when thou fastest' contain an implied command.*

Of a sad countenance. — Strictly, of sullen look, moroseness of affected austerity rather than of real sorrow.

They disfigure their faces. — The verb is the same as that translated 'corrupt' in verse 19. Here it points to the unwashed face and the un-

---

[51] Joseph Addison Alexander, *The Gospel According to Matthew* (New York: Charles Scribner, 1861), 176.

trimmed hair, possibly to the ashes sprinkled on both, that men might know and admire the rigorous asceticism." [52]

Charles Rosenbury Erdman —Verses 17-18: *"Very popular with the Jews among whom Christ lived, was that of fasting. If this is practiced in order to show to God our sorrow for sin; or if it is involved in our devotion to his service, it is right and commendable; but if it is employed as a means of winning the approval and praise of men, it is hypocrisy and pretense. Jesus insists that fasting, and all forms of self-denial, should be in secret; we are not to parade our sacrifices; we are not to make capital out of our devotion. We are to have regard only to the Father who is in secret, who sees in secret and who surely will reward."* [53]

---

[52] Charles John Ellicott, *A New Testament Commentary for English Readers (Matthew-John), Volume 1* (Edinburg: The Calvin Translation Society, 1884), 26.

[53] Charles Rosenbury Erdman, *The Gospel of Matthew: An Exposition* (Philadelphia: The Westminister Press, 1920), 56.

Righteousness and Ordinary Earthly Things

Here We Have Presented the Requirements For Christ's Followers to Trust God Completely and Seek His Kingdom First and Foremost.
Matthew 6:19-34

Andrew Fuller —Verses 19-20: *"'Lay not up for yourselves treasures.' The Lord here proceeds to a variety of counsels, and all upon things in common life. The inhabitants of this busy world are taken up in accumulating something which may be called their own, and in setting their hearts upon it rather than upon God. So common is this practice that, provided they do not injure one another, it insures commendation rather than reproach. 'Men will*  *praise thee when thou doest well to thyself.' Hence we are in greater danger of this sin than of most others. In opposition to this, we are directed to 'lay-up treasures in heaven.' Not that the heavenly inheritance is the reward of our doings: but, believing in Christ, and setting our affections on things above, where Christ sitteth at the right hand of God, everything we do in his name, whether it be to the poor, or any others, for his sake, turns to our account. Heavenly enjoyment accumulates, as we in this way make much of it. It is thus that, in 'giving alms, we provide ourselves bags which wax not old, a treasure in the heavens which faileth not.' Men commonly choose a safe place to lay up their treasure. It is said that many millions, during the late depredations on the continent, have been placed in the English funds; and no wonder. But still there is nothing secure in this world. If we would place our treasure in a bank where no marauder cometh, it must be 'hid with Christ in God.'*

From this passage, some have seriously concluded that it is forbidden us in any case to add to our property. To be consistent, however, they should not stop here, but go on to 'sell what they have and give it to the poor: 'for the one is no less expressly required than the other. But this were to overturn all distinctions of rich and poor, and all possession of property, which is contrary to the whole current of Scripture. To lay up 'treasures upon earth' is to trust in them, or make them our chief good, instead of using them as a means of glorifying God and doing good in our generation. This is evident from the reason given against it, that, 'where our treasure is, there will our heart be also.' The Lord prospered David; yet David's treasures were not in this world. On the contrary, he was distinguished from 'men of this world, who had their portion in this life;' declaring, 'As for me, I will behold thy face in righteousness: I shall be satisfied when I awake in thy likeness.' If, however, our treasure be in heaven, we shall not be eager to lay up worldly wealth; but rather to lay out that which God entrusts in our hands for promoting the good of his cause, and the well-being of mankind." [54]

William Burkitt —Verse 21: "21 For where your treasure is, there will your heart be also. Observe here, 1. Something implied, namely. That every man has his treasure; and whatsoever or wheresoever that treasure is, it is attractive, and draws the heart of a man unto it: for every man's treasure is his chief good. 2. Something permitted; namely, the getting, possessing, and enjoying, of earthly treasure, as an instrument enabling us to do much good. 3. Something prohibited; and that is, the treasuring up of worldly wealth, as our chief treasure: Lay not up treasures on earth; that is, take heed of an inordinate affection to, of an excessive pursuit after, of a vain confidence and trust in, any earthly comfort, as your chief treasure. 4. Here is something commanded; but lay up for yourselves treasures in heaven: treasure up those habits of grace, which will bring you to an inheritance in glory: be fruitful in good works, laying up in store for yourselves a good foundation against the time to come, that ye may lay hold of eternal life. Observe, 5. The reasons assigned, 1. Why we should not lay up our treasure on earth; because all earthly

---

[54] Andrew Fuller, *The Complete Works of Rev. Andrew Fuller: Expository Discources and Notes-Sermons and Sketches-Circular Letters-Letters on Systematic Divinity-Thoughts on Preaching-Life of Pearce-Apology for Missions-Tracys and Essays-Reviews-Answers to Queries-Fugitive Pieces, Volume 2* (Boston: Lincoln, Edmands & Company, 1833), 102.

treasures are of a perishing and uncertain nature, they are subject to moth and rust, to robbery and theft; the perishing nature of earthly things ought to be improved by us, as an argument to sit loose in our affections towards them. 2. The reason assigned why we should lay up our treasure in heaven, is this: because heavenly treasures are subject to no such accidents and casualties as earthly treasures are but are durable and lasting. The things that are not seen are eternal. The treasures of heaven are inviolable, incorruptible, and everlasting. Now we may know whether we have chosen these things for our treasure, by our high estimation of the worth of them, by our sensible apprehension of the want of them, by the torrent and tendency of our affection towards them, and by our laborious diligence and endeavours in the pursuit of them. Where the treasure is, there will the heart be also." [55]

Albert Barnes —Verses 22-23: *"22, 23. The light of the body. The sentiment stated in the preceding verses — the duty of fixing the affections on heavenly things — Jesus proceeds to illustrate by a reference to the eye. When the eye is directed singly and steadily towards an object, and is in health, or is single, everything is clear and plain. If it vibrates, flies to different objects, is fixed on no one singly, or is diseased, nothing is seen clearly. Everything is*  *dim and confused. The man, therefore, is unsteady. The eye regulates the motion of the body. To have an object distinctly in view, is necessary to correct and regulate action. Ropedancers, in order to steady themselves, fix the eye on some object on the wall, and look steadily at that. If they should look down on the rope or the people, they would become dizzy and fall. A man crossing a stream on a log, if he will look across at some object steadily, will be in little danger. If he looks down on the dashing and rolling waters, he will become dizzy, and fall. So, Jesus says, in order that the conduct may be right, it is important to fix the affections on heaven. Having the affections there — having the eye of faith single, steady, unwavering — all the conduct will be correspondent. Single. Steady, devoted to one object. Not confused, as*

---

[55] William Burkitt, *Expository Notes, with Practical Observations, on the New Testament of our Lord and Saviour Jesus Christ, Volume 1* (Philadelphia: Thomas Wardle, 1835), 29-30.

persons' eyes are when they see double. *Thy body shall be full of light.* Your conduct will be regular and steady. All that is needful to direct the body is that the eye be fixed right. No other light is required. So, all that is needful to direct the soul and the conduct is, that the eye of faith be fixed on heaven, that the affections be there. *If, therefore, the light that is in thee.* The word *light,* here, signifies the mind, or principles of the soul. *If this be dark, how great is that darkness!* The meaning of this passage may be thus expressed: The light of the body, the guide and director, is the eye. All know how calamitous it is when that light is irregular or extinguished, as when the eye is diseased or lost. So, the light that is in us is the soul. If that soul is debased by attending exclusively to earthly objects — if it is diseased, and not fixed on heaven — how much darker and more dreadful will it be than any darkness of the eye! Avarice darkens the mind, obscures the view, and brings in a dreadful and gloomy night over all the faculties." [56]

Thomas Boston —Verses 24: "'No man can serve two masters: for either he will hate the one and love the other; or else he will hold to the one and despise the other. Ye cannot serve God and mammon.' Mammon is thought to be an idol, which the heathens reckoned to be the god of money and riches. Now, says Christ, you cannot serve them both; if you would have the Lord for your God, and serve him, you must renounce mammon. We cannot serve two gods or masters: if but one require our whole time and strength, we cannot serve the other." [57]

John Charles Ryle —Verses 25: "He forbids us to keep up an anxious spirit about the things of this world. Four times over He says, "take no thought.' About life, — about food, — about clothing,— about the morrow, 'take no thought." Be not over careful. Be not over-anxious.

---

[56] Albert Barnes, *Explanatory and Practical, on the Gospels Designed for Sunday School Teachers and Bible Classes, Volume 1* (Philadelphia: Harper & Brothers, 1840), 86-87.

[57] Samuel M'Millan and Thomas Boston, *The Whole Works of the Late Reverend and Learned Mr. Thomas Boston, Minister of the Gospel at Etterick, Volume 1* (Aberdeen: George & Robert King, 1848), 137.

Prudent provision for the future is right. Wearing, corroding, self-tormenting anxiety is wrong.

He reminds us of the providential care that God continually takes of everything that He has created. Has He given us 'life?' Then He will surely not let us want anything necessary for its maintenance. Has He given us a 'body?' Then He will surely not let us die for want of clothing. He that calls us into being, will doubtless find meat to feed us.

He points out the uselessness of over-anxiety. Our life is entirely in God's hand. All the care in the world will not make us continue a minute beyond the time which God has appointed. We shall not die till our work is done." [58]

Archibald Thomas Robertson —Verses 26-27: "The birds of the heaven. Luke (12:24) says 'ravens.' This beautiful illustration applies to the sustenance of life. The birds get food. Jesus does not, of course, mean for his illustration to be pressed too far. He is not advocating reckless indifference and idleness. Even the birds have to work for their food. Are not ye. If God takes the birds into his plans, he will his children. It is the argument from the less to the

greater. Here again we must not put into the mouth of Christ what he does not expressly say. He assumes work and discountenances anxiety and distrust. He by no means advocates indifference to oppression and needless social inequalities, the problem of predatory wealth and of the unemployed. But the man in real straits must not lose sight of God his Father.

Stature. The word is ambiguous. It is used for 'stature' in Lk. 19:3 and for 'age' in Jn. 19:21; Heb. 11:11. In the ancient writers it is more common for 'age.' In verse 26 Jesus has been discussing the 'life,' and 'age' would be the idea if he still has that point in mind. In verse 28 he turns

---

[58] J. C. Ryle, *Expository thoughts on the Gospels: For Family and Private Use, Volume 1 (St. Matthew)* (New York: Robert Carter & Brothers, 1857), 59.

to the 'body,' and 'stature' would best harmonize with that conception. It all turns on whether vs. 27 belongs to the discussion of vs. 26 or of vs. 28. The word 'cubit' certainly suits 'stature' better than 'age,' though a cubit added to one's height would be no little increase. Before one is fully grown, he does grow in stature, but not by 'anxiety.'" [59]

John Gill —Verse 28: *"And why take ye thought for raiment. Having exposed the folly of an anxious and immoderate care and thought, for food to support and prolong life, our Lord proceeds to show the vanity of an over concern for raiment: consider the lilies of the field or the flowers of the field, as the Arabic version reads it, the lilies being put for all sorts of flowers. The Persic version mentions both rose and lily; the one being beautifully clothed in red, the other in white. Christ does not direct his hearers to the lilies, or flowers which grow in the garden which receive some advantage from the management and care of the gardener; but to those of the field, where the art and care of men were not so exercised: and besides, he was now preaching on the mount, in an open place; and as he could point to the fowls of the air, flying in their sight, so to the flowers, in the adjacent fields and valleys: which he would have them look upon, with their eyes, consider and contemplate in their minds, how they grow; in what variety of garbs they appear, of what different beautiful colours, and fragrant odours, they were; and yet they toil not, or do not labour as husbandmen do, in tilling their land, ploughing their fields, and sowing them with flax, out of which linen garments are made: neither do they spin; the flax, when plucked and dressed, as women do, in order for clothing; nor do they weave it into cloth, or make it up into garments, as other artificers do."* [60]

Alexander Maclaren —Verse 29: *"'Solomon in all his glory was not arrayed like one of these,' there is an instance of God's giving more than barely enough; He lavishes beauty, He touches the flower into grace,*

---

[59] A. T. Robertson, *Commentary on the Gospel According to Matthew* (New York: The MacMillan Company, 1911), 111-112.

[60] John Gill, *An Exposition of the New Testament in Which the Sense of the Sacred Text is Given, Volume 1* (London: Mathews & Leigh, 1809), 65.

and decks waste places with fairness, and 'so' clothes the grass of the field that we may learn that a fair spirit, who delights in a fair creation, a bountiful spirit who gives with both hands, presides over all things, and divides His gifts to men." [61]

Lyman Abbott —Verse 30: *"The grass of the field .... cast into the oven. Weeds and grass were and still are used in the East as fuel. Ovens were constructed in various ways: sometimes of earth; sometimes a pit, lined with cement, served the purpose; sometimes baking was done simply on stones heated by fire previously kindled on them. The oven here mentioned was a large round pot of earthen or other materials, two or three feet high, narrow towards the top. This being first heated by a fire made within, the dough or paste was spread upon the sides to bake, thus forming their cakes. In all these cases the fuel was cast into the oven, and when the oven was sufficiently heated, was raked out again to make room for the bread, after the manner in vogue in the use of the old brick oven. The verse recurs to the underlying reason for not being anxious; God who cares for birds and flowers much more cares for us his children. Oh ye of little faith. He cares even for the untrusting (2 Tim. 2:13)."* [62]

Philip Doddridge —Verse 31: *"Be not ye therefore any more distracted and torn in pieces (as it were) with anxious and unbelieving thoughts, saying, What shall we eat, or what shall we drink? How is it we shall be provided for, or what shall we wear, in the remainder of our lives? (For it is really beneath your character as my disciples, thus to distress yourselves on this account: the heathen, who are strangers to the promises of God's covenant and to*

---

[61] Alexander McClaren, *The Gospel of St. Matthew, Volume 1* (London: Hodder & Stoughton, 1892), 101.

[62] Lyman Abbott, 1876, *The New Testament with Notes and Comments: Accompanied with Maps and Illustrations (Matthew and Mark)* (New York: A. S. Barnes & Company, 1876), 107.

the hopes of his glory, do indeed seek after all these things: and it is no wonder that their minds are taken up with them: but you have greater business to employ you, and higher hopes to animate and encourage you;) for you may be assured that as your Father knows that you need all these things while you dwell in the body, he will not fail to provide them for you." [63]

John Calvin —Verse 32: *"For all those things the Gentiles seek. This is a reproof of the gross ignorance, in which all such anxieties originate. For how comes it, that unbelievers never remain in a state of tranquillity, but because they imagine that God is unemployed, or asleep, in heaven, or, at least, that he does not take charge of the affairs of men, or feed, as members of his family, those whom he has admitted to his friendship. By this comparison he intimates, that they have made little proficiency, and have not yet learned the first lessons of godliness, who do not behold, with the eyes of faith, the hand, of God filled with a hidden abundance of all good things, so as to expect their food with quietness and composure. Your heavenly Father knoweth that you have need of those things: that is, "All those persons who are so anxious about food, give no more honour, than unbelievers do, to the fatherly goodness and secret providence of God."* [64]

John Heyl Vincent —Verse 33: *"Seek ye first — Not only seek, it is 'seek first.' 1. First in point of time; morning conditions the day; twisted sapling gives of very necessity the gnarled and crooked tree. Even so youth's best time for religious decision, and generally wisdom for all of us, is religion first in the life, first in the week, first every day. 2. Religion must be first in point of effort. We give energy, and care, and diligence to things according to*

---

[63] Philip Doddridge, *The Works of the Rev. P. Doddridge*, Volume 6 (Leeds: Edward Baines, 1804), 229.

[64] John Calvin, *A Commentary on a Harmony of the Evangelists, Matthew, Mark, and Luke*, Volume 1 (Edinburg: The Calvin Translation Society, 1836), 343.

their importance; even so, then, as eternity is longer than time, and the soul more precious than the body, in such proportion religion must be preferred to all other concerns that may engage us. 3. Religion must be first in the sense of being supreme; it is not a question of mere preference, but of rule. —J. M. Stott. Not with any reference to seeking all these things after our religious duties; that is, beginning with prayer days of avarice and worldly anxiety, but make your great object, as we say, your first care. —Alford. The kingdom of God—Be God's, wholly and singly; and let neither covetousness on the one hand, nor mistrustful anxiety on the other, distract your attention or divide your service. — Vinet. His righteousness — Not here the forensic righteousness of justification, but the spiritual purity inculcated in this discourse. —Alford. 1. The aim of true life— 'The kingdom of God.' 2. The business of true life — Seeking the kingdom. 3. The inclusiveness of true life — All these things shall be added. — W. W. Wythe. Shall be added — They shall be cast in as an overplus, or as small advantage to the main bargain; as paper and pack thread are given where we buy spice and fruit, or an inch of measure to an ell of cloth. —Trapp. [65]"

David Thomas —Verse 34: *"'To-morrow shall take thought for the things of itself.' To-morrow will bring its own blessings; the sun will rise and shine, the air will breathe its life, the refreshing streams will flow, the earth will bud and bloom, and all nature will work beneath its God to-morrow, to supply the wants of man and beast. To-morrow will have a God as yesterday and to-day, opening His liberal hand and supplying the wants of every living thing.*

The future has its trials. 'Sufficient unto the day is the evil thereof.' To-morrow will have its trials as well as blessings: afflictions, pains, sorrows, vexations, disappointments, are in the morrow. Our morrow will not dawn as the morrow of heaven upon a sinless world, and therefore will have its trials. The expression 'sufficient unto the day is the evil thereof,' implies that not only every day has its trials, but that anxieties for the future augment the trials of the present. There is a

---

[65] J. H. Vincent, *The Lesson Commentary on the International Lessons for 1880* (London: Elliot Stock, 1879), 65-66.

tendency in man to antedate his sorrows as well as his joys. Antedated trials are imaginary, and such trials are often the worst. First, they may never actually occur. Imagination is a busy prophet, it is ever speaking 'of things to come,' but its auguries are seldom fulfilled. It has not only promised us joys that have never come but threatened us with evils that happily have never come to pass. How often have men looked on to some day in the future which they expected would be most disastrous to them; they have seen the looming clouds gather and blacken and felt the most terrible foreboding. The day came, and there was no storm. Secondly, when imaginary trials occur, they are seldom so severe as was expected. Imagination exaggerates everything, it magnifies and colours all it touches. Thirdly, there is no consolation promised under imaginary trials. They are not calamities, they are crimes. Fourthly, they augment the real trials of life. Every day has its own trials. Providence has mercifully spread our trials over the whole period of life, to every day its own. By over anxiety we bring them together, and thus impose burdens on ourselves which often bar us from the pleasures and incapacitate us for the duties of the present. 'Let us not,' says an old writer, 'pull that upon ourselves all together at once, which Providence has wisely ordered to be borne by parcels.'

> Be it ours to walk the changing path of life, identifying a God with loving every object along the road, and ever cherishing a child-like confidence in the parental providence, which is over us, yes, and before us too. Let our steps be free and firm, let us bear the passing storms of the day, ever anticipating the sunshine of tomorrow." [66]

---

[66] David Thomas, *The Genius of the Gospel: A Homiletical Commentary on the Gospel of St. Matthew* (London: Dickinson & Higham, 1873), 69-70.

Matthew 7

Christ Admonishes Thoughtless Judgment
Jesus Warns Against Judging Others and the Calling His Redeemed People to Perfection.
Matthew 7:1-6

Charles Haddon Spurgeon —Verses 1-2: *"Judge not, that ye be not judged. For with what judgment ye judge, ye shall be judged: and with what measure ye mete, it shall be measured to you again. Use your judgment, of course: the verse implies that you will judge in a right sense. But do not indulge the criticizing faculty upon others in a censorious manner, or as if you were set in authority, and had a right to dispense judgment among your fellows. If you impute motives, and pretend to read hearts, others will do the same towards you. A hard and censorious behaviour is sure to provoke reprisals. Those around you will pick up the peek measure you have been using and measure your corn with it. You do not object to men forming a fair opinion of your character, neither are you forbidden to do the same towards them; but as you would object to their sitting in judgment upon you, do not sit in judgment upon them. This is not the day of judgment, neither are we his Majesty's judges, and therefore we may not anticipate the time appointed for the final assize, nor usurp the prerogatives of the Judge of all the earth.*

Surely, if I know myself aright, I need not send my judgment upon circuit to try other men; for I can give it full occupation in my own Court of Conscience to try the traitors within my own bosom." [67]

---

[67] Charles H. Spurgeon, *The Gospel of the Kingdom: A Popular Exposition of the Gospel According to Matthew* (London: Passmore & Alabaster, 1893), 40-41.

Charles Frederick Schaeffer —Verses 3-5: *"And why beholdest thou the mote that is in thy brother's eye, but considerest not the beam that is in thine own eye?*

A. Mote — any particle of straw, wood, etc., a splinter here representing a defect or fault. —B. Beam — a rafter, a heavy piece of timber supporting the roof. 'It is an image of a sin that is immeasurably greater than one represented by a mote.'—Luther. —C. Thine own eye. The eye represents the moral and religious character and conduct. The sense is: Thou hast faults of thine own; thou hast a better opportunity to read thine own heart and judge of its iniquity than thou hast to ascertain the state of thy neighbor's heart. Thy own faults should therefore appear to thee far more heinous than those of thy neighbor. His motives, which thou canst not know, may be in reality less censurable than thine own. (Comp. 23:24, 'thy brother'—thy equal in knowledge, etc.).

Or how wilt thou say to thy brother, let me cast out the mote out of thine eye; and lo, the beam is in thine own eye?

How wilt — how canst thou presume to say, etc. (Luke 6:42). The sense is: Thou dost contract guilt already by thy neglect of strict self-examination, and by an unwarranted condemnation of another; thy iniquity is still greater when thou dost hypocritically assume the character of a well-meaning friend and adviser, while thy heart is filled with self-righteousness and pride; these vices exclude all knowledge of thyself, and all sincere regard for the welfare of thy brother (see Rom. 2:21-23, 'Can the blind lead the blind?' Luke 6:39).

Thou hypocrite, first cast out the beam out of thine own eye; and then shalt thou see clearly to cast out the mote out of thy brother's eye.

Thou hypocrite — who pretendest to be wiser and better than another, study the divine law, and ascertain first thy own sinful state. Then only, when the light of truth guides thee, and when thou hast, as an humble believer, found joy and peace (Rom. 15:13), mayest thou, with the wisdom which faith imparts, 'see clearly' how to teach transgressors (Ps. 51:12, 13) and to strengthen thy brethren (Luke 22:32; see Rom. 2:17-24)." [68]

John Heyl Vincent —**Verse 6:** *"Give not — These exhortations to gentleness are followed very appropriately by the command to beware of the other extreme, that is, an indiscriminate pouring out of holy things from want of judgment. He who forbids our judging (which decides man's culpability) commands us to form an opinion, (which marks only the state.) This latter is absolutely necessary for the child of God, in order to distinguish the false from*  *the true. —Olshausen. The holy, a technical term for the sacrificial meats laid upon the altar of God. Of these meats no unclean man was permitted to eat; how much less a dog; to the Jew the dog was odious and unclean; even to touch him was to become unclean. —S. Cox. Unto the dogs — The dog was never a pet or a favorite among the Jews. They lived, and still live in oriental cities, in packs, half wild, generally without masters or owners, and barely tolerated as scavengers. Both Bible of vileness and uncleanness (Lev. 11.7; Prov. 11.22; Matt. 15.27; Phil. 3.2; Rev. 22.15.) —Abbott. Neither cast ye your pearls — It has been suggested that the figure alludes to the resemblance of pearls with peas and acorns. Certain it is that the swine touch with their snouts everything resembling food. As this casting of pearls before swine, however foolish, must have had some show of reason, it may, perhaps, represent an attempt of satisfying their cravings, and such, indeed, is the true character of laxity; it prostitutes what is highest and holiest to satisfy the animal and the devilish propensities of man.—Lange. Before swine —Tho other part of the similitude is of a different character, and belongs entirely to the swine, who having cast to them pearls, something like their natural food, whose value is inappreciable by them, in fury trample them with their feet, and, turning against the donor, rend him with their tusks. —Alford. Rend you — Such, then, are the twofold consequences: that which is holy, with all its treasures, is lost in iniquity, and more; while its unfaithful and vile administrators also perish*

---

[68] Charles F. Schaeffer, *Annotations of the Gospel According to St. Matthew, Part I– Matthew I-XV* (New York: The Christian Literature Company, 1895), 159-160.

in their sin. —Lange. Apostles and bishops must not commit the office of the ministry to a wicked man. No sacred deposit, or responsibility, or even principle, (symbolized by pearls,) must be imparted to an unfit man. No doctrines or religious experiences must be brought before an incapable sensualist. In fine, in imparting the official trusts and the truths of the Gospel, we must discern men's moral qualities, and deal with them accordingly. —Whedon. Good men should so study the judicial capability of bad men as to cause themselves not to be misjudged and injured. Adaptation to men, places, and things, requires consummate judgment; the savage might be more pleased with a brass button than with a thousand-pound note. He who would give a telescope to a wild barbarian would be deranging the true relations of things, as would he also who excluded all but the blind from the galleries of art. Men must be met on their own intellectual plane, and judgment must be so far exercised as not to confound fools with philosophers, or to regard the toys of children as the accouterments of warriors. —Parker. This, however, does not imply that we are not to seek.'" [69]

---

[69] J. H. Vincent, *The Lesson Commentary on the International Lessons for 1880* (London: Elliot Stock, 1879), 68-69.

True Prayer and the Golden Rule
Jesus Continues to Emphasized the Importance of Prayer, Noting His People Ought Always Pray.
Matthew 7:7-12

William Nast —Verses 7-12: *"To whom and for what we ought to pray is self-evident, the three different expressions constitute a beautiful gradation in enforcing intense, continual prayer. The exhortation to seek refers to that old promise recorded (Deut. 4:29) that God shall be found by all that seek with their whole heart and their whole soul. To him that asks, the object of his desire appears as something that he is destitute of; to him that seeks, as something*  *that he has lost; to him that knocks, as something that is locked up. Verse 8 greatly confirms the promises of verse 7. The words 'Everyone that asketh,' etc., are intended as a reproof and remedy for that lack of faith, or little faith, which scarcely dares to claim any promise for its own prayer. At the same time, they also intimate that he who does not ask, seek, or knock, will receive nothing from the Lord. Ask, become a beggar at the gate of grace, and ask with humble confidence. Seek: thou hast lost thy God, thy soul, thy paradise; seek, therefore, carefully and at the right place. Knock: be in earnest, knock hard, and again and again.*

Verse 9 ought to be translated, 'Which of you is a man? he (that is) will certainly not give a stone if his son asks him for bread,' etc., our Lord declaring thereby, that he that does is no longer a man, a human being. What man will be so unfeeling and cruel against his entreating child to give it for a cake of bread a hard stone, or for a fish a noxious serpent, or, as Luke adds, a venomous scorpion for an egg? Ye, then, know how to give good gifts to your children; ye do so from that impulse of nature which God has implanted in you. How much more your Father in heaven! It is worthy of note that the Lord substitutes for the mere refusal — the offering of a stone or of a serpent. Stier sees in this a new idea. Parents know how to distinguish between what is good and evil for their children, giving them only what is good for them, and with-

holding whatever might be hurtful; how much more will God act thus! What is hurtful to us, or what is not conducive to our real welfare, he will withhold from us, even if we should most urgently ask him for it. To us, in our short-sightedness, it may seem as necessary as a piece of bread to a hungry child; but God in his infinite wisdom sees, that if he should give it to us it would prove as useless as a stone to a child, or as dangerous as a serpent, and for this reason he withholds it.

If ye then being evil. According to Stier these words contain one of the strongest proofs that all men are naturally depraved, and that our Lord is more than a mere man, inasmuch as he exempts himself in this declaration from all other men. — The argument is: If in men who, without exception, are depraved and evil, and who lack true, unchanging love, nevertheless paternal affection is so strong that they give good gifts to their children, how much more will our Heavenly Father, whose love is infinitely stronger, whose very nature is to give, grant good gifts (Luke xi, 13, says 'the Holy Ghost') unto them that ask him!.

In this so-called golden rule, the Lord comprehends the whole law, as far as it has a bearing on our conduct toward our fellowmen. This rule is easy to be understood, universally acknowledged to be reasonable and just, and most salutary in its effects, and would, if it were universally observed, remove most of the sufferings of mankind. The consecutive particle, 'therefore,' refers not to what immediately precedes, but to all the precepts laid down by our Savior throughout his whole sermon. It is worthy of note, that both the rabbins and heathen philosophers had this rule in a negative form, and so it is still proverbially used, 'do not do unto others what you do not wish them to do unto you.' But the Lord bringing it nearer the conscience, says: 'All things whatsoever ye would that men should do to you, do ye even so to them.' He that does to his neighbor everything that he may in justice and mercy demand of him, has fulfilled the law. The commandment enjoins love from a pure heart; but this purity of heart is found only where sin is pardoned through faith, by the grace of him who has come to fulfill the law and the prophets, (chap, v, 17) and in this sense the Lord says: 'This is the law and the prophets.'" [70]

---

[70] William Nast, *A Commentary on the Gospels of Matthew and Mark* (Cincinnati: Poe & Hitchcock, 1864), 277-278.

Social Morality and the Divine View of Life

Jesus Teaches Of Two Gates, Two Ways, Two Destinations And Two Groups Of People.
Matthew 7:13-14

Harvey Goodwin —Verses 13-14: *"13. Enter ye in at the strait gate: for wide is the gate, and broad is the way, that leadeth to destruction, and many there be which go in there at: 14. Because strait is the gate, and narrow is the way, which leadeth unto life, and few there be that find it.*

One of the most solemn given by our Lord. S. Luke reports a saying, which may possibly have been in reality the same as this which is given by S. Matthew, and which at all events throws light upon the passage: S. Luke tells us that some one asked Christ whether they were few who would be saved, and that in reply He said, Strive to enter in at the strait or narrow gate! The Words of our Lord therefore may be concluded to contain a warning of the difficulty of entering into the Heavenly kingdom; the gate of it is narrow, easy to miss, not wide enough to admit a sinner who wishes to take his burden of sin or his cloke of hypocrisy or the like impediments with him. And as if to shew that he really meant what He said, the Lord added, Few there be that find this narrow gate, yes, few; perhaps few absolutely, but certainly few as compared with the number of those, who walk in the broad way which leads to destruction.

Two things may be particularly noted in these words of our Lord. In the first place, we cannot but observe the weighty practical kind of teaching which He adopts. Here is a great truth which it concerns all men to know; the way of destruction is easy, the way of life is difficult; one it is hard to miss, the other it is not so easy to find; this being so, our Lord tells us that it is so in all simplicity; He neither exaggerates the evils of the case nor hides them, but He testifies in plain solemn language to the fact, which unhappily our own experience proves to be too true, namely, that the way of sin and self is easy, and the way of the fear of God much the contrary.

In the second place, we cannot but observe the reason why our Lord revealed to us this truth, or rather why He testified to us concerning it: it is not to encourage any spirit of curiosity or inquisitiveness concerning the way in which our neighbours may be going, but it is for the purpose of inciting us to take the wise course; enter ye—do not ask whether other people are entering, but enter ye — even if there should be no others following the narrow path of life, do not ye go on the broad road of destruction: it will be no consolation to you, if you are destroyed, to know that many thousands have perished with you. So practical is the teaching of Christ; He never encourages us to pry into mysteries, He never unveils for the satisfaction of our curiosity the secrets of the unseen world; but He deals with us as creatures of awful responsibility and of infinite destiny, and dealing with us as such He tells us in plain language of those things which concern our peace." [71]

---

[71] Harvey Goodwin, *A Commentary on the Gospel of S. Matthew* (Cambridge: Deighton & Company, 1857), 130-131.

The Elements of Moral Character and Its Fruit
Jesus' Teaching of False Prophets.
Matthew 7:15-20

Joseph Addison Alexander —**Verse 15:** *"Beware of false prophets, which come to you in sheep's clothing, but inwardly they are ravening wolves. The danger of mistake as well as difficulty, hinted in the last words of the verse preceding, would suggest, by obvious association, the necessity of guidance, with its natural correlative, the risk of being misled to destruction. This fearful peril would be greatest where the guides possessed authority and enjoyed the confidence of those whom they conducted. This was really the case with the religious leaders of the Jews, the Scribes and Pharisees, to whom there seems to be immediate reference, although, instead of being named they are described in terms derived from the Old Testament, where false religious teachers, claiming a divine authority, are called false prophets. As prediction of the future is not even the original and primary functions of a prophet, but authoritative teaching in the name of God, the phrase is perfectly appropriate to those here characterized by it. At the same time, it admits of a wider application to false teachers of a later date, confirmed by the constant use of prophet in relation to the Christian church. Beware, the verb employed above in 6:1, and there explained. Of, away from, so as to avoid connection or communication with them. Which come, not such of them as come, as if this were only true of some false prophets, but who as such (or because they are such) come. This is the true force of the pronoun here used, which is carefully distinguished in Greek usage from the ordinary relative. The highly figurative terms which follow are derived from the habits of pastoral life, with which many of the hearers were familiar from experience or observation. As the wolf is the natural enemy of sheep, it is elsewhere used as a figure for the cruel enemies of Christ's flock (see below, on 10, 16 and compare John 10, 12. Acts 20, 29). But the stronger and more*

complete figure of a wolf disguised as a sheep, conveys the idea of deceit and treachery combined with cruelty and savage fierceness. In sheep's clothing, or garments of sheep, does not mean in literal sheepskins, in allusion to the dress of the old prophets; first, because this custom is assumed without proof; then, because this explanation would either destroy the correspondence of the clauses, or require us to understand the whole description literally, which would be absurd. The true sense is, that these false prophets come to (or approach) the people, claiming to be like themselves in point of harmlessness, simplicity, and intimate connection with the church or chosen people, often represented as the flock of God; while in reality, within, inside (Vulg. intrinsecus), as distinguished from the outside appearance or profession, they are wolves, destructive enemies, and ravening (i. e. eagerly seizing and devouring) wolves. Within, or more exactly, from within, which may either be taken as equivalent to inside, an interpretation justified by classic usage, or explained more strictly as suggesting the idea of movement or action from within (ab intra). In appearance they are sheep, but by the actions which proceed from within, or by their inward character, as wrought out in their conduct, they are seen to be rapacious wolves. This severe accusation was repeated and sustained at length near the close of our Lord's ministry." [72]

James Morison —Verse 16: "From their fruits ye shall know them: Watch their conduct, watch their character. If they are bad men, unprincipled, selfish, or acting in private at variance with their professional acting in public, then pay no regard to their teaching. It was a sad inversion of the Saviour's rule that was made by Jerome, when he interpreted it thus, Ye shall know them by their doctrines. And yet Calvin held the same idea. He says, 'under the fruits the kind of teaching holds the chief place.' Trapp echoes the notion; he says, 'by their fruits, that is, chiefly by their doctrines.' Such an interpretation of our Saviour's rule formed the sheet anchor of the Inquisition. Happily Luther took the right view; and so did Zuingli; and so did Augustin, who says that the fruits referred to are the fruits of

---

[72] Joseph Addison Alexander, *The Gospel According to Matthew* (New York: Charles Scribner, 1861), 206-207.

the Spirit mentioned in Gal. v. 22, 23. The question is, Are these fruits present? or are they absent? Do men gather grapes of thorns, or figs of thistles? No. Such incongruities do not occur; although in the spiritual sphere of things there are multitudes of thistle plants and thorn bushes that have figs and grapes stuck on. Hence occasionally you may get grapes on thorns and figs on thistles. You may occasionally get good teaching from bad men. They have learned it and stuck it on; but it is by no means the outgrowth of their own experience and character." [73]

George Whitefield Clark —Verses 17-18: *"Even so. What is true of thorns and thistles is true of every kind of tree. Good tree. A tree of good quality, and good for bearing. Corrupt tree. Literally, rotten; which is hardly the meaning here, since rotten or decayed trees do not usually bear fruit. It rather means, bad in quality, in opposition to good. Thus, the same Greek word is applied to fish in Ch. 13:48 and translated bad. Jesus here states a general fact, that good trees do produce good fruit; and bad, worthless trees, evil fruit.*

The case stated still stronger. Not only is it a general fact, but it must be so. It is impossible for a good tree, from its very nature, to bring forth evil fruit, or for a bad, noxious tree to bring forth good fruit. The heart of man is depraved, and if he is unrenewed, his depravity must affect his whole conduct. This is especially true of false religious teachers. Their depravity will affect their whole faith and practice, and will show itself in their actions, their instructions, in a selfish and wicked spirit, and in false doctrine, 1 John 4:1-3." [74]

Philip Doddridge —Verses 19-20: *"Every tree that bringeth not forth good fruit, is hewn down and cast into the fire. And therefore, by the way, to prevent such false pretenders to religion from being a lasting incumbrance and mischief, they shall assuredly be overtaken by the*

---

[73] James Morrison, *A Practical Commentary on the Gospel According to St. Matthew* (London: Hodder & Stoughton, 1895), 112.

[74] George W. Clark, *A Peoples Commentary: The Gospel of Matthew, A Popular Commentary Upon A Critical Basis, Especially Designed for Pastors and Sunday Schools* (Philadelphia: American Baptist Publication Society, 1896), 103-104.

 *righteous judgment of God; and as you see that every tree which, after a competent trial, beareth not good fruit, how fair and flourishing soever it may seem, is cut down and cast into the fire; such too will be the end of hypocritical professors and ungodly men, which it becomes you all seriously to consider. Wherefore by their fruits ye shall know thein. Upon the whole it will be found that there is now a difference in men's characters correspondent to the great difference to be made in their future estate; so that I had reason to say, that you shall generally know them by their fruits; the disguise will fall off in an unguarded moment, and it will be your wisdom to observe and improve the signal."* [75]

---

[75] Philip Doddridge, *The Works of the Rev. P. Doddridge, Volume 6* (Leeds: Edward Barnes, 1804), 214-236.

Man's Religions, and Their Testing Day

Jesus Addresses Man's Religion of Profession, Merit, Hearing, Doing — And The Day Of Testing.
Matthew 7:21-27

William Burkitt —Verses 21-23: *"21 Not every one that saith unto me, Lord, Lord, shall enter into the kingdom of heaven; but he that doeth the will of my Father which is in heaven. 22 Many will say to me in that day, Lord, Lord, have we not prophesied in thy name? and in thy name have cast out devils? and in thy name done many wonderful works? 23 And then will I profess unto them, I never knew you: depart from me, ye that work iniquity. Not everyone, that is, Not any one, that saith, Lord, Lord, that is, that owneth me by way of profession, by way of prayer, and by way of appeal, shall be saved; but he that doeth the will of my Father, sincerely and universally. Learn hence, 1. That multitudes at the great day shall be really disowned by Christ as none of his servants, that did nominally own him for their Lord and Master: many that have now prophesied in his name, shall then perish in his wrath: many that have cast out devils now, shall be cast out to devils then: such as have now done many wonderful works, shall then perish for evil workers. Note, 2. That a bare name and profession of Christianity, without the practice of it, is a very insufficient ground to build our hopes of heaven and salvation upon. A profession of faith, and purposes of obedience, without actual obedience to the commands of God, will avail no person to salvation. 3. That gifts, eminent gifts, yea, extraordinary and miraculous gifts, are not to be rested in, or depended upon, as sufficient evidences for heaven and salvation. Gifts are as the gold which adorns the temple, but grace is like the temple that sanctifies the gold."* [76]

---

[76] William Burkitt, *Expository Notes, with Practical Observations, on the New Testament of our Lord and Saviour Jesus Christ, Volume 1* (Philadelphia: Thomas Wardle, 1835), 34.

 **William Bruce —Verses 24-25:** *"Therefore, whosoever heareth these sayings of mine, and doeth them, I will liken him unto a wise man; and every one that heareth these sayings of mine, and doeth them not, I will liken him unto a foolish man. The whole difference between the wise and the foolish, and between the eternal consequences of wisdom and folly, consists in one thing, and is described by one word, and that one word is Doeth. This word holds a most prominent place in the whole of the Scriptures of truth, and an all-important place in the economy of the religious life. To do or not to do decides the question of order and disorder, of weakness and power, of salvation and condemnation, of life and death. Doing is the use and end of religion. Hearing the Lord's sayings, which includes knowing and understanding them, is but a means to an end, and that end is to do them. To do what we hear is wisdom; to hear and not do is folly. Wisdom and folly in Scripture do not mean intellectual, but moral states. Wisdom is not knowledge, but the right use of it; folly is not the absence of knowledge, but its abuse. He that heareth these sayings of mine, and doeth them, I will liken him to a wise man. Let us see what this man did as an evidence of his wisdom. He built his house upon a rock. The expressive word edification means building up and has been borrowed to express the idea of practical education, as a building up of the mind in knowledge and virtue. In this sense it is used in Scripture. The only difference is that the materials here are spiritual, and the building is not for time but for eternity. Everyone builds in this world the house in which he shall live forever. The materials of this house are the truths of the Word, and these may be built up by practical wisdom into a holy habitation, in which grace and truth may dwell together — yea, in which the Lord himself, by his love and wisdom, may take up his abode, according to his own divine promise: 'If a man love me, he will keep my words; and my Father will love him, and we will come unto him, and make our abode with him.' But the stability of the house depends on the foundation on which it is built. The wise man builds his house upon a rock. This rock is eminently the Lord himself. A rock, in Scripture is the symbol of truth; and the Lord is called a rock, as being the truth itself; and he is especially the Rock of Ages as the truth manifested — the Word made flesh. Faith in this*

Truth — or this Truth held in faith — is the rock on which the wise man builds his house. It is that of which the Lord declared to Peter, after his ever-memorable confession, 'Thou art the Christ,' — 'On this rock I will build my church.' And the house which the Christian builds upon this foundation is the church in him.

The advantage of building the house upon a rock our Lord describes by expressive figures. And the rain descended, and the floods came, and the winds blew, and beat upon that house; and it fell not: for it was founded upon a rock. The power of resisting trials and temptations is the great advantage which results from a faith which rests on the foundation of the Lord Jesus Christ. There is no regeneration without temptation. Temptation is the trial of our faith. Temptation confirms a true faith and overturns a false one. A true faith is not only a faith in the truth, but a faith that is true — sincere. A true faith is one that is of the thought from affection, and a false faith is one that is of the thought without affection. A true faith, therefore, not only resists in temptation, but is increased and confirmed by it. The temptations to which faith is subjected are described by the storm that fell upon the house. And no images could more expressively depict the danger to which the mind is exposed by the trials and temptations of life than that which threatens the house by the combined action upon it of the rain, the flood, and the wind. The temptation arising from false suggestions are meant by the rain; for rain, when it falls upon the earth in gentle and fructifying showers, is the expressive symbol of truth; when it beats upon the house, and threatens it with destruction, is the equally expressive symbol of falsity. And as the subject of the Lord's words is the foundation of a true faith, the temptations come from what is opposite to, and tends directly to invalidate the truth, and destroy faith in it. But not only does the rain descend, but the floods come. Rain is that kind of temptation that comes in gradually-increasing torrents of false suggestions; but floods are those temptations that arise from the accumulation of such false suggestions, and when they come in a body, like an inundation of waters, bear down every thing that is not capable of the greatest resistance. The wind indicates that kind of temptation that flows into the thoughts — for wind is more subtle than water — and are the stormy winds that sweep over the mind like a tornado and threaten to root up and cast down everything before it. But there is one object that resists them all — the house that is founded upon a rock. The church of the Lord that is built in the human mind upon the rock of a living faith — against it the very gates of hell shall not prevail. And these temptations of which our Lord here speaks are induced by the powers of darkness, and are the means which the spirits of darkness employ for the purpose of effecting their purpose of destroying the soul, by pulling down what the Saviour has built up. But the assurance which the Saviour gives to his faithful ones is, that having built their faith upon him as its foundation, all the combined powers of the kingdom of darkness, in the severest temptations, will not be able to overturn it. And it fell not: for it was founded upon a rock." [77]

John Guyse —Verses 26-27: "On the other hand, whoever hears my instructions, but disregards them, and never puts them into practice, may very properly be compared to an inconsiderate careless man, who builds his house upon a loose and sandy foundation; for when storms and rains beat upon the superstructure, it is easily overturned and utterly destroyed, as having no good bottom to keep it from sinking and falling in its own ruins: So the mere, empty, hypocritical professor of religion, has nothing to support or secure him in an hour of temptation and danger, much less in the day of death and judgment; but must inevitably perish, and that with great aggravation of his sin and folly, and to his dreadful disappointment forever." [78]

---

[77] William Bruce, *Commentary on the Gospel According to St. Matthew* (London: Frederick Pitman, 1867), 197-199.

[78] John Guyse, *The Practical Expositor: or An Exposition of the New Testament in the Form of a Paraphrase, Volume 1 (Matthew and Mark)* (Edinburgh: Ogle, Allardice & Thomson, 1818), 50.

The World's Greatest Teacher
Our Notice of Christ As The World's Greatest and Highest Teacher.
Matthew 7:28-29

Matthew Henry —Verses 28-29: *"In the two last verses, we are told what impressions Christ's discourse made upon the auditory. It was an excellent sermon; and it is probable that he said more than is here recorded; and doubtless the delivery of it from the mouth of him, into whose lips grace was poured, did mightily set it off. Now, 1. They were astonished at his doctrine: it is to be feared 'that few of them were brought to follow him; but for the present, they were filled with wonder. Note, It is possible for people to admire good preaching, and yet to remain in ignorance and unbelief; to be astonished, and yet not sanctified. 2. The reason was because he taught them as one having authority, and not as the Scribes. The Scribes pretended to as much authority as any teachers whatsoever, and were supported by all the external advantages that could be obtained, but their preaching was mean, and flat, and jejune: they spake as those that were not themselves masters of what they preached: the word did not come from them with any life or force; they delivered it as a school-boy says his lesson; but Christ delivered his discourse, as a judge gives his charge. He did indeed, dominari in concionibus — deliver his discourses with a tone of authority; his lessons were laws; his word a word of command. Christ, upon the mountain, showed more true authority, than the Scribes in Moses's seat. Thus when Christ teaches by his Spirit in the soul, he teaches with authority. He says. Let there be light, and there is light."* [79]

---

[79] Matthew Henry, *An Exposition of the Old and New Testament*, Volume 5 (Philadelphia: Edward Barrington & George D. Haswell, 1825), 85-86.

An Ordinary Commentary by Ordinary Men: The Sermon on the Mount

Commentaries

Abbott, Lyman, 1876, *The New Testament with Notes and Comments: Accompanied with Maps and Illustrations (Matthew and Mark)* (New York: A. S. Barnes & Company, 1876).

Alexander, Joseph Addison, *The Gospel According to Matthew* (New York: Charles Scribner, 1861).

Barnes, Albert, *Explanatory and Practical, on the Gospels Designed for Sunday School Teachers and Bible Classes, Volume 1* (New York: Harper & Brothers, 1840).

Belcher, Joseph, *The Complete Works of Rev. Andrew Fuller: With A Memoir of His Life, Volume 1* (Philadelphia: American Baptist Publication Society, 1845).

Bonhoeffer, Dietrich, *Cost of Disciples* (New York: MacMillan Publishing Company, 1979).

Boston, Thomas, *The Whole Works of the Late Reverend and Learned Mr. Thomas Boston, Minister of the Gospel at Etterick, Volume 1* (Aberdeen: George & Robert King, 1848).

Broadus, John Albert, *An American Commentary on the New Testament. Commentary on the* Gospel of Matthew (Philadelphia: American Baptist Publication Society, 1886).

Burkitt, William, *Expository Notes, with Practical Observations, on the New Testament of our Lord and Saviour Jesus Christ, Volume 1* (Philadelphia: Thomas Wardle, 1835).

Bruce, William, *Commentary on the Gospel According to St. Matthew* (London: Frederick Pitman, 1867).

Calvin, John, *A Commentary on a Harmony of the Evangelists, Matthew, Mark, and Luke, Volume 1* (Edinburg: The Calvin Translation Society, 1836).

Chambers, Oswald, *Studies in the Sermon on the Mount* (London: Simpkin Marshall, LTD, 1900).

Clark, George Whitefield, *The Bible Work (or Bible Readers Commentary) The New Testament, in Two Volumes, Volume 1* (New York: Funk & Wagnalls, 1889).

Clarke, Adam, *The New Testament of Our Lord Jesus Christ, Volume 1, Matthew to the Acts* (New York: Lane & Scott, 1850).

Crosby, Howard, *The New Testament, With Brief Explanatory Notes or Scholia* (New York: Charles Scribner, 1863).

Doddridge, Philip, *The Works of the Rev. P. Doddridge, Volume 6* (Leeds: Edward Barnes, 1804).

Ellicott, Charles John, *A New Testament Commentary for English Readers (Matthew-John), Volume 1* (Edinburg: The Calvin Translation Society, 1884).

Erdman, Charles Rosenbury, *The Gospel of Matthew: An Exposition* (Philadelphia: The Westminister Press, 1920).

Fuller, Andrew, *The Complete Works of Rev. Andrew Fuller: Expository Discources and Notes-Sermons and Sketches-Circular Letters-Letters on Systematic Divinity-Thoughts on Preaching-Life of Pearce-Apology for Missions-Tracys and Essays-Reviews-Answers to Queries-Fugitive Pieces, Volume 2* (Boston: Lincoln, Edmands & Company, 1833).

Doddridge, Philip, *The Works of the Rev. P. Doddridge, Volume 6* (Leeds: Edward Barnes, 1804).

Gill, John, *An Exposition of the New Testament in Which the Sense of the Sacred Text is Given, Volume 1* (London: Mathews & Leigh, 1809).

Goodwin, Harvey, *A Commentary on the Gospel of S. Matthew* (Cambridge: Deighton, Bell & Company, 1857).

Guyse, John, *The Practical Expositor or An Exposition of the New Testament, in the Form of a Paraphrase, Volume 1* (Edinburgh: Ogle, Allardice & Thomson, 1818).

Hastings, James, *The Great Texts of the Bible, Volume 8 (Matthew)* (Edinburgh: T. & T. Clark, 1910).

Henry, Matthew, *An Exposition of the Old and New Testament, Volume 5* (Philadelphia: Edward Barrington & George D. Haswell, 1825).

Hill, Daniel Harvey, *A Consideration of the Sermon on the Mount* (Philadelphia: William S. & Alfred Martein, 1858).

Jamieson, Robert, Fausett, A. R., Brown, David, *A Commentary, Critical, Experimental, and Practical, on the Old and New Testaments, Volume 5 (Matthew-John by David Brown)* (Philadelphia: L. P. Lippincott, 1866).

Luther, Martin, *Commentary on the Sermon on the Mount* (Philadelphia: Lutheran Publication Society, 1892).

Manton, Thomas, *The Works of Thomas Manton, Volume 5* (London: James Nibet & Company, 1871).

McClaren, Alexander, *The Gospel of St. Matthew, Volume 1* (London: Hodder & Stoughton, 1892).

McIntyre, William, *Exposition of the Sermon on the Mount, Matthew 5-7* (Edinburgh: Johnstone & Hunter, 1854).

Morgan, George Campbell, *The Gospel According To Matthew* (New York: Fleming H. Revel, 1939).

Morrison, James, *A Practical Commentary on the Gospel According to St. Matthew* (London: Hodder & Stoughton, 1895).

Nast, William, *A Commentary on the Gospels of Matthew and Mark* (Cincinnati: Poe & Hitchcock, 1864).

Patrick, Patrick, *Critical Commentary and Paraphrase on the Old and New Testament and the Apocrypha, Volume 4 (Gospels to Epistles)* (Philadelphia: Carey & Hart, 1845).

Rice, Edwin Wilbur, *Commentary on the Gospel According to Matthew* (Philadelphia: The American Sunday-School Union, 1897).

Richmond, Legh, *A Selection from the Writings of the Reformers and Early Protestant Divines of the Church of England, Volume 5* (London: John Hatchard, Bookseller to Her Majesty, 1810).

Robertson, Archibald Thomas, *Commentary on the Gospel According to Matthew* (New York: The MacMillan Company, 1911).

Schaeffer, Charles Frederick., *Annotations of the Gospel According to St. Matthew, Part I–Matthew I-XV* (New York: The Christian Literature Company, 1895).

Schaff, Philip, *A Popular Commentary on the New Testament, Volume 1* (New York: Charles Scribner's Sons, 1891).

Spurgeon, Charles Haddon, *The Gospel of the Kingdom: A Popular Exposition of the Gospel According to Matthew* (London: Passmore & Alabaster, 1893).

Sumner, John Bird, *A Practical Exposition of the Gospels of St. Matthew and St. Mark, in the Form of Lectures* (London: Hatchard & Son, 1831).

Thomas, David, *The Genius of the Gospel: A Homiletical Commentary on the Gospel of St. Matthew* (London: Dickinson & Higham, 1873).

Henry Thornton, *Family Prayers, and Prayers on the Ten Commandments, to Which Added A Commentary of the Sermon Upon the Mount* (New York: Stanford & Swords, 1846).

Vincent, John Heyl, *The Lesson Commentary on the International Lessons for 1880* (London: Elliot Stock, 1879).

Bible and Other Sources

The Holy Bible, Updated New American Standard Bible (Grand Rapids: Zondervan Publishing House, 1999), 969.

Hastings, James, *A Dictionary of the Bible: Dealing with its Language, Literature and Content Including the Biblical Theology, Volume 1* (A-FEAST) (New York: Charles Scribner's Sons, 1898).

www.ingramcontent.com/pod-product-compliance
Lightning Source LLC
Chambersburg PA
CBHW052113110526
44592CB00013B/1599